DATE DUE		

Biofuels

Leanne Currie-McGhee

Energy and the Environment

ReferencePoint
Press®

San Diego, CA

© 2010 ReferencePoint Press, Inc.

For more information, contact:
ReferencePoint Press, Inc.
PO Box 27779
San Diego, CA 92198
www.ReferencePointPress.com

Picture credits:
Cover: Istockphoto.com
AP Images: 16
Istockphoto.com: 11
Steve Zmina: 31–34, 47–49, 61–64, 77–79

LIBRARY OF CONGRESS CATALOGING-IN-PUBLICATION DATA

Currie-McGhee, L. K. (Leanne K.)
Biofuels / by Leanne K. Currie-Mcghee.
    p. cm. — (Compact research)
Includes bibliographical references and index.
ISBN-13: 978-1-60152-078-4
ISBN-10: 1-60152-078-6
1. Biomass energy—Juvenile literature. I. Title.
TP339.C87 2009
333.95'39—dc22

2009004289

Contents

Foreword

❝ Where is the knowledge we have lost in information? ❞

—T.S. Eliot, "The Rock."

As modern civilization continues to evolve, its ability to create, store, distribute, and access information expands exponentially. The explosion of information from all media continues to increase at a phenomenal rate. By 2020 some experts predict the worldwide information base will double every 73 days. While access to diverse sources of information and perspectives is paramount to any democratic society, information alone cannot help people gain knowledge and understanding. Information must be organized and presented clearly and succinctly in order to be understood. The challenge in the digital age becomes not the creation of information, but how best to sort, organize, enhance, and present information.

ReferencePoint Press developed the *Compact Research* series with this challenge of the information age in mind. More than any other subject area today, researching current issues can yield vast, diverse, and unqualified information that can be intimidating and overwhelming for even the most advanced and motivated researcher. The *Compact Research* series offers a compact, relevant, intelligent, and conveniently organized collection of information covering a variety of current topics ranging from illegal immigration and deforestation to diseases such as anorexia and meningitis.

The series focuses on three types of information: objective single-author narratives, opinion-based primary source quotations, and facts and statistics. The clearly written objective narratives provide context and reliable background information. Primary source quotes are carefully selected and cited, exposing the reader to differing points of view. And facts and statistics sections aid the reader in evaluating perspectives. Presenting these key types of information creates a richer, more balanced learning experience.

For better understanding and convenience, the series enhances information by organizing it into narrower topics and adding design features that make it easy for a reader to identify desired content. For example, in *Compact Research: Illegal Immigration*, a chapter covering the economic impact of illegal immigration has an objective narrative explaining the various ways the economy is impacted, a balanced section of numerous primary source quotes on the topic, followed by facts and full-color illustrations to encourage evaluation of contrasting perspectives.

The ancient Roman philosopher Lucius Annaeus Seneca wrote, "It is quality rather than quantity that matters." More than just a collection of content, the *Compact Research* series is simply committed to creating, finding, organizing, and presenting the most relevant and appropriate amount of information on a current topic in a user-friendly style that invites, intrigues, and fosters understanding.

Biofuels at a Glance

Biofuels and the Obama Energy Agenda

In February 2009, President Barack Obama signed the American Recovery and Reinvestment Act, a $787 billion economic stimulus bill that includes $14 billion in tax incentives for biofuel facilities and other renewable energy sources. Additionally, the Obama administration's "New Energy for America" plan sets out long-term energy goals such as ensuring that 25 percent of America's electricity comes from renewable sources by 2025 and investing $150 billion over 10 years to stimulate private clean energy projects. The how, what, and when of such spending has prompted considerable debate.

Biofuels and Fossil Fuels

The world depends on fossil fuels for the majority of its energy needs. Fossil fuels are nonrenewable. For this reason, interest in renewable energy sources such as biofuels has increased.

Renewable Resources

Biofuels are made from renewable plant matter and other living material. These are called biomass. Currently, the main sources of biomass are corn, sugarcane, palm oil, and soybeans.

Types of Biofuels

The most common biofuels are biodiesel, ethanol, and biomethane. These can be used to fuel vehicles, provide energy for electricity, and heat buildings.

Biofuel Use

Worldwide biofuel production tripled from 2000 to 2007. In 2000 the world produced 4.8 billion gallons (18 billion L) of biofuel. In 2007 world biofuel production was 16 billion gallons (60.6 billion L).

Biofuels and Carbon Dioxide

Fossil fuels emit carbon dioxide when they burn. Carbon dioxide contributes to global warming. Biofuel crops, such as corn and sugarcane, absorb carbon dioxide when they grow. This helps to offset the carbon dioxide emitted when biofuels are burned.

Production Issues

Fossil fuels are used in the production and transportation of biofuels. This reduces biofuels' overall environmental benefits.

Using Land

Large areas of grasslands and rain forests are often cleared for growing biomass crops, prompting concerns about environmental impact.

Rising Food Costs

Many biofuels are made from crops, such as corn, that are also used as food. Some claim that diverting food to biofuels contributed to record food costs in 2008. The rise in prices resulted in food crises throughout the world.

Second-Generation Biofuels

Scientists have found that biofuels can be made from nonfood crops such as switchgrass and algae. However, the technology for doing this is still young, and commercial production plants are several years away.

Overview

> **❝Biomass offers America tremendous opportunity to use domestic and sustainable resources to provide its fuel, power, and chemical needs from plants and plant-derived materials.❞**
>
> —U.S. Department of Energy.

> **❝Biofuels have been hailed as a green alternative to oil by some, but in the U.S. . . . it has been criticized for making food more expensive and being environmentally unfriendly.❞**
>
> —Juliette Jowit, environmental editor for London's *Observer*.

Fossil fuels, which include natural gas, petroleum, and coal, provide the majority of the world's energy for cars, electricity, and heating. A major problem is that fossil fuels are made from nonrenewable resources, which are resources that cannot be replaced once used. Additionally, fossil fuels are being depleted at a fast rate. Some experts estimate that the world will use twice the energy it does today in 2035. Unless changes are made, to meet this demand experts estimate that oil requirements will nearly double; the use of natural gas would need to expand by 120 percent, and coal use would need to increase by nearly 60 percent.

Because fossil fuels are nonrenewable, countries are investigating alternative energy sources to decrease fossil fuel use. Examples of alternative energy sources are wind, solar, and biofuels. Biofuels are the most commonly used alternative fuel source.

Biofuels are made from renewable resources. Renewable resources are those that can be replaced after they are used. Biofuels are mainly made from crops such as corn or soybeans that can easily be grown again. Biofuels can provide fuel for vehicles; they can be used in making electricity and for heating homes. Currently biofuels only provide a small percentage of the world's energy. In the United States biofuels meet about 3 percent of the country's energy needs.

Many countries want to increase biofuel usage, but they must overcome obstacles. One obstacle is that it takes a large amount of plant material to produce a small amount of biofuels. For example, it takes about 26 pounds (11.8 kg) of corn to make 1 gallon (3.8 L) of ethanol. Another obstacle is cost; most biofuels must be transported by trucks and other vehicles to fueling stations instead of the less expensive method of transport through pipelines.

What Are Biofuels?

A biofuel is any fuel that is made from biomass. Biomass is material that comes from renewable biological material such as plants. Plants are renewable because they can be grown again once used. To be considered a biofuel, fuel must be made from at least 80 percent renewable materials.

> **Because fossil fuels are non-renewable, countries are investigating alternative energy sources to decrease fossil fuel use.**

Biomass is made into fuels by different methods. The oldest way is simply to burn the biomass. For years people burned wood to produce heat for warmth and cooking. The problem with burning biomass is that much energy is wasted in the process.

A more efficient use of biofuels is to convert the biomass's carbohydrates into fuel. This is done through chemical processes. Chemical processes can convert the carbohydrates into sugars and the sugars into alcohol, a liquid fuel. Often this type of fuel is used for cars. Other chemical processes can make biofuels from vegetable oils and animal fats. These can also be used to fuel vehicles.

Another way to use biomass is to create gas from organic material such as animal manure or sewage. Biomethane is produced by the biological breakdown of organic matter in the absence of oxygen. This is done in machines called anaerobic digesters, which are air-tight, oxygen-free containers that are fed an organic material such as animal manure or food scraps. The digester creates biomethane from decaying organic material. This gas can be used for electricity, water heating, and other functions.

Biofuels Past and Present

Biofuels were the first fuel people ever used. Early people burned wood, a biofuel, to heat and to cook. Over the years, people discovered more innovative ways to use biofuels. When cars were first invented, scientists developed ways to fuel them with biofuels. Henry Ford planned to use biofuels for the cars he produced in the late 1920s. However, he changed his mind when he found it was easier and cheaper to buy gas made from petroleum, a fossil fuel. It was also easier and cheaper to use fossil fuels for electricity and heating. For that reason, biofuels did not become a major energy source and fossil fuels did.

> To be considered a biofuel, fuel must be made from at least 80 percent renewable materials.

Biofuel use has increased during times of scarcity, however. Many countries turned to biofuels during the oil crisis of 1973. During this year the Organization of Petroleum Exporting Countries (OPEC), an organization of 13 oil-producing countries, controlled two-thirds of the world's oil reserves. OPEC said it would not ship oil to the United States and other countries that supported Israel in the Yom Kippur War of 1973. The United States relied on OPEC for the majority of its petroleum. Because of the embargo, the country experienced gas shortages. The United States and other countries turned to ethanol, a biofuel typically made from corn or sugarcane, because they could produce it themselves. They mixed it with gasoline to stretch supplies. However, as soon as the embargo was over, countries turned back to gasoline.

In recent years, countries have started to use biofuels on a long-term basis. One reason is that oil prices have been on the rise. Crude oil consistently rose from 2001, when it averaged $23.12 per barrel for the year, to 2008, when it averaged $94.45 for that year. Countries would like to reduce their dependence on OPEC and make their own fuels. To do so some countries, such as Brazil, the United States, and the United Kingdom, have mandated biofuel use. As a result, biofuel use has been rising around the world. For example, in 2004 the world produced over 10.77 billion gallons (40.8 billion L) of ethanol. This rose to 13.48 billion gallons (51 billion L) in 2006.

Ethanol

Ethanol is one of the most commonly used biofuels. It is made from the sugar of plants such as corn and sugarcane. These plants are commonly used because the sugar in them is easily extracted and converted to ethanol.

All plants make sugar through photosynthesis. When plants are growing they undergo photosynthesis, a process where sunlight is used

Corn is harvested for ethanol production. Ethanol is one of the most commonly used biofuels. It is made from the sugar of plants such as corn and sugarcane. These plants are commonly used because the sugar in them is easily extracted and converted to ethanol.

to make sugar. As plants grow, carbon dioxide and water enter them. The plants also absorb sunlight that then chemically reacts with the carbon dioxide and water to make sugar. The sugar is extracted from the plants and then undergoes fermentation, which is a process that changes the sugars to an alcohol called ethanol.

Most of the ethanol made in the United States is used to fuel cars. In 2007 there were 110 factories in the United States producing ethanol. The plants produced enough ethanol to meet 3.5 percent of America's car fuel needs.

> " The problem with biofuels is that even using all the current biomass available, they cannot totally replace fossil fuels. "

The United States makes most of its ethanol from corn. The main problem with corn-based ethanol is the amount of corn needed to produce fuel. Even if the United States used all of its corn to make ethanol, it would only be able to replace about 12 percent of the gasoline the nation uses for cars.

Sugarcane produces more ethanol per crop than corn, but it can only be grown in tropical climates. Brazil, which has a tropical climate, grows thousands of acres of sugarcane each year. Brazil is one of the largest producers of ethanol in the world. Brazil has replaced 40 percent of its gas with ethanol. Eighty-five percent of cars sold in Brazil are "flex-fuel" cars, meaning they can either burn ethanol or traditional gasoline. In 2008 ABC News reported that Brazil was energy independent, meaning it no longer had to rely on foreign markets for oil.

Biodiesel

Biodiesel is another type of biofuel. It is made by converting vegetable oils and animal fats into fuels. Typical vegetable oils used to make biofuels are rapeseed, soybean oil, and palm oil. The process used to convert these oils into biodiesel is called transesterification. During this process, glycerin is separated from the fat or vegetable oil. Taking out the glycerin leaves methyl esters, the chemical name for biodiesel.

Biodiesel's main use is to fuel diesel vehicles. Biodiesel can be used alone or mixed with traditional diesel. The engines of vehicles that run on regular diesel do not have to be adapted to run on a biodiesel-diesel mix.

Europe uses more diesel cars than the United States, so it relies more on biodiesel than ethanol as a biofuel. In Europe most biodiesel is produced from rapeseed oil. In 2006 Europe made 134,000 barrels of biodiesel per day. By 2008 this rose to 226,000 barrels per day. The biodiesel is mixed with regular diesel fuel and used in cars and buses all across Europe.

Although ethanol is the preferred biofuel for U.S. vehicles, the country's biodiesel use is growing. The United States increased its biodiesel consumption from 25 million gallons (95 million L) in 2004 to 78 million gallons (295 million L) in 2005. This was a 300 percent increase in just one year. Much of this increase was due to the Energy Policy Act of 2005. The act required fuel producers to make a minimum amount of biofuels.

> " Overall global biofuel production has tripled from 4.8 billion gallons (18 billion L) in 2000 to about 16 billion gallons (60.6 billion L) in 2007. "

Biodiesel has an added benefit: It can be used to produce electricity. "Biodiesel is finding new life as a fuel in generators and turbines to produce electricity," writes Anduin Kirkbride McElroy for *Biodiesel* magazine. "The application is gaining a lot of interest in states where traditional electricity from coal is too dirty or too remote."[1]

Biomethane

Biomethane is becoming more popular as a biofuel. It can be used in place of natural gas for generating electricity, heating homes, and powering vehicles. Unlike ethanol and biodiesel, which are both liquid biofuels, biomethane is a gas. It is made from the waste products of animals, crops, or even sewage.

Biomethane is produced by the biological breakdown of the waste. The breakdown of the waste occurs through anaerobic digestion. Microbes break down manure into biomethane. The captured methane can then be used in different ways.

Landfills hold waste that can be broken down into biomethane. As of December 2007 approximately 445 landfill gas energy projects, where landfill waste is used to make biomethane, operated in the United States. The generated electricity was either used on site or sold to companies that operate power grids, systems of high-tension cables that distribute electrical power throughout a region.

> **Plants absorb carbon dioxide, which reduces the amount of greenhouse gases trapped in the atmosphere.**

Solid Biofuels

Solid biofuels are used throughout the world. Wood is the most common solid biofuel. In developing countries, whose people generally have little money, wood is easy to find and is often burned for cooking and heating. The main problem with this is that wood burning produces smoke and soot that cause health problems, including asthma, and it pollutes the air with carbon monoxide.

Burning wood can create electricity. This is done in a machine called a combustion boiler. The burning of wood in a boiler creates steam, and the steam turns a turbine. The turbine is connected to an electric generator and causes the generator's shaft and armature to spin. This spinning produces an electric current.

Some companies in the lumber industry have even begun using wood waste to power their operations. UPM is one of the world's largest forest products companies. It produces printing and specialty papers, paper products, and wood products in 16 countries. The production of these products results in wood waste. Since the company was established in 1995, it has increasingly used this wood waste from its production to make some of the company's electricity. Wood-based renewable fuels and heat account for 55 percent of the company's needs.

Can Biofuels Reduce Dependence on Fossil Fuels?

In 2008 the Department of Energy reported that approximately 85 percent of the United States's energy demand is met by fossil fuels. Fossil fuels are nonrenewable and decreasing at a rapid rate. It is difficult for scientists to estimate how long fossil fuels will last because there are sources, such as oil deposits, that have not yet been found. However, all agree that fossil fuels are limited. "There is lots of oil out there," said Karl Kurz, vice president of marketing and minerals for Anadarko Petroleum. "But it's a finite resource; we can't get around that. Eventually, you're going to get to the point where there's not any more to find."[2]

Biofuels are considered a good alternative to fossil fuels because they are made from renewable sources. Biomass will not run out. Another advantage of biofuels is that most countries can produce biofuels on their own rather than having to rely on other countries to supply their energy needs. Additionally, biofuels are thought to be more environmentally friendly than fossil fuels.

For these reasons, biofuels are on the rise throughout the world. The United States is the world's largest biofuel producer, and its production is increasing. In 2008 the United States produced 572,000 barrels of corn ethanol a day, up from 333,000 per day in 2006. Overall global biofuel production has tripled from 4.8 billion gallons (18 billion L) in 2000 to about 16 billion gallons (60.6 billion L) in 2007.

The problem with biofuels is that even using all the current biomass available, they cannot totally replace fossil fuels. This is because large amounts of biomass are needed to significantly decrease fossil fuel use. According to one estimate, if the United States used all of its corn for ethanol, leaving none for food, it would only be able to make enough ethanol to replace 15 percent of gasoline and diesel. For biofuels to have a significant effect on fossil fuel usage, scientists believe that more efficient ways to create biofuels are needed.

Sweden's Success

Sweden is working toward becoming an oil-free country. The high oil prices of the 1970s prompted Sweden to start using more alternative fuels. Since then, it has actively used wind, solar, nuclear, and biofuels in its quest to reduce dependence on fossil fuels.

Biofuels provide much of the country's transportation fuel. One-fifth of the cars in the capital city of Stockholm run on alternative fuels, mostly sugarcane ethanol imported from Brazil. The Swedish government's flexible-fuel vehicle (FFV) fleet, the largest in Europe, uses E85 fuel, which is 85 percent ethanol and 15 percent gasoline. That fleet grew from 717 vehicles in 2001 to 116,695 in 2008.

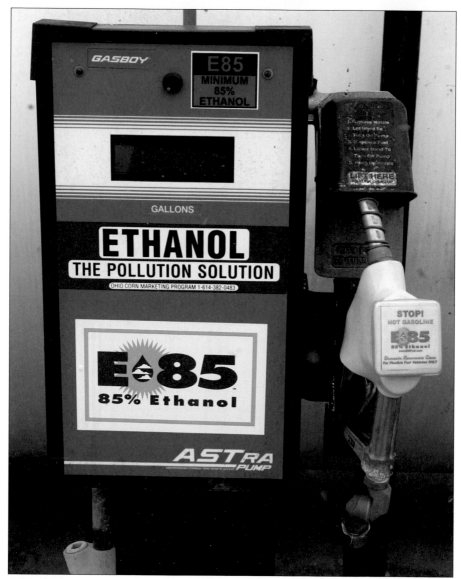

This fuel pump in Ohio offers E85 fuel, which is 85 percent ethanol and 15 percent gasoline. In 2008 there were 1,900 filling stations in the United States that carried E85.

In 1970 biofuels provided 9 percent of Sweden's energy needs. By 2006 biofuels provided 17 percent of Sweden's total energy needs. This was the country's highest percentage of energy provided by an alternative source. The increased use of biofuels has helped Sweden reduce its fossil fuel use. From 1970 to 2006 Sweden decreased its oil use by over

40 percent. Sweden believes that with increased biofuel use and other alternative fuels, it can stop oil imports by 2020.

How Do Biofuels Affect the Environment?

Many scientists believe that biofuels are less harmful to the environment than fossil fuels. Fossil fuels emit carbon dioxide when they are burned. Carbon dioxide is a greenhouse gas. Most scientists believe greenhouse gases are a major cause of global warming. Greenhouse gases trap heat from the sun in the Earth's atmosphere, raising the Earth's temperature. Many scientists believe that global warming is the cause of rising sea levels, melting icecaps, and significant worldwide climatic changes, such as more frequent and more powerful hurricanes.

> In 2008 Mexicans marched in their capital of Mexico City, claiming the diversion of corn to fuel was creating a food crisis.

Environmentalists claim that biofuels are better for the environment than fossil fuels because biofuels come from plants that are growing today. Plants absorb carbon dioxide, which reduces the amount of this greenhouse gas trapped in the atmosphere. Although biofuels produce carbon dioxide when they burn, the amount of carbon dioxide absorbed by the plants they are made from balance out these emissions.

Not all people believe that biofuels are a better environmental choice than fossil fuels. This is because fossil fuels are used during the production and transport of biofuels. As Fred Krupp and Miriam Horn write:

> There is a notable irony associated with biofuels production. In pursuit of climate-friendly transport fuel, the industry has generated increased demand for coal—the most polluting of the fossil fuels. Throughout the Midwest and Plains states, ethanol developers are either building their own coal-fired boilers to generate the heat and pressure they need, or buying electricity from local co-ops that, in turn, are planning new coal-fired power plants.[3]

Does Biofuel Production Threaten the World Food Supply?

According to the International Monetary Fund, world food prices rose 10 percent in 2006. This was mainly because of price increases in corn, wheat, and soybeans—all of which are considered food staples for countries worldwide. The rise in prices led to food crises, or extreme shortages of food, in many countries.

Some say increasing demand for biofuel is partly to blame for the rise in food prices. Corn, wheat, and soybeans are the most common crops used in the making of biofuels. In hopes of cashing in on the demand for biofuel crops, many farmers have stopped growing crops for food and have started growing crops for fuel. The result has been shortages of certain foods and higher food prices.

In 2007, 75,000 Mexicans marched in their capital of Mexico City because of a major hike in corn tortilla prices. Many claimed the diversion of corn to fuel was creating the food crisis. In some areas of Mexico, the price per kilogram of tortillas rose from an American equivalent of 63 cents in January 2006 to between $1.36 and $1.81 in January 2007. With a minimum wage of $4.60 a day, this resulted in Mexican families having to spend as much as a third of their income on tortillas, a main staple of their diets. "Right or wrong that was when blame settled on biofuels for the surge in food prices,"[4] writes Arthur Max of the Associated Press. In 2008 the World Bank calculated that 70 to 75 percent of the food price rises were due to biofuels.

> Universities, corporate research firms, and governments are spending millions of dollars for the research on how to make effective and cost-efficient biofuels from woody or grassy biomass.

Others argue that biofuels contributed little to the rising food prices. The U.S. Department of Agriculture (USDA) said that using food crops for biofuels resulted in only 3 percent of global food price increases. Instead, the USDA blamed the food price increases on the high cost of oil used for transporting food around the world.

What Is the Future of Biofuels?

Concerns about using food crops for fuel have prompted research into the use of nonfood crops in the making of biofuels. For instance, some companies are turning discarded cooking oil into vehicle fuel.

Carlo Bakker owns a tiny biofuel operation in South Africa called World Mobile Plants. He has a mini-refinery that is loaded into a 40-foot (12 m) shipping container on a flatbed truck. Bakker drives around South Africa and makes biodiesel from people's used cooking oil. He hopes eventually to use organic household waste, such as animal and human sewage, to make biofuel. Bakker says that one mobile unit can make 260,000 gallons (984, 207 L) of biodiesel a year. He sells it at $3.79 a gallon, which is equivalent to regular diesel prices.

Scientists are finding other ways to make biofuels from nonfood crops. Universities, corporate research firms, and governments are spending millions of dollars for the research on how to make effective and cost-efficient biofuels from woody or grassy biomass. The complex starches in the biomass must be reduced to sugar, which can be converted into biofuel. Converting the starches into sugars is the difficult part. Because of the difficulty, it is also expensive. For this reason, commercial production plants for these fuels are still years away. However, scientists and environmentalists have great hopes that these and other sources will provide a major amount of fuel in the future.

Can Biofuels Reduce Dependence on Fossil Fuels?

66 Fossil fuels are variably distributed and all geopolitical regions have, and for a while will, satisfy their energy demands with a significant component of fossil fuels. 99

—Scott Tinker, director of the Bureau of Economic Geology at the University of Texas at Austin.

66 The problem is, fossil fuels are non-renewable. They are limited in supply and will one day be depleted. There is no escaping this conclusion. 99

—Eric McLamb of Ecology Global Network.

Fossil fuels provide most of the world's energy. These fuels include coal, petroleum, and natural gas. Fossil fuels are made from the remains of dead plants and animals. These remains were fossilized after exposure to heat and pressure in the Earth's crust over a period of hundreds of millions of years.

There are different ways to extract fossil fuels from the Earth's crust. Oil, which is processed into fuels, is found deep in the ground. Oil companies dig wells to the oil then pump it out. A refinery changes the oil into products like gasoline, jet fuel, and diesel fuel. The oil can also be burned and the steam used to turn turbines that make electricity. Natural gas is found near oil. It is pumped out, just like oil, and sent to large pipelines. Through the pipes the gas goes to homes so people can cook food and heat their homes. Natural gas is also burned in factories and power plants to make electricity. Coal is found near the Earth's surface and extracted by mining. Trains typically transport coal to power plants, where it is burned to make steam. The steam turns turbines, which produce electricity.

The world's dependence on fossil fuels is troubling to many because fossil fuels are nonrenewable resources. It takes millions of years to form fossil fuels. Once used, fossil fuels are gone. A major problem is that new sources of fossil fuels are being found at a lesser rate than the rate at which they are being used. According to the Global Education Project, the world currently finds one barrel of oil for every four consumed. Although fossil fuels are in no immediate danger of being completely used up, experts agree that the world needs to lessen dependence on them because world energy demands are going to increase.

America's Addiction

The United States is home to 5 percent of the world's population, yet consumes 26 percent of the world's energy. Fossil fuels provide approximately 85 percent of its energy needs. The United States uses fossil fuels in many ways. Approximately 30 percent of U.S. energy demand is for transportation. American vehicles get most of their energy from oil. The heating sector also makes up 30 percent of U.S. energy demand. Heating sources are primarily oil and natural gas. The electricity sector represents 40 percent of U.S. energy demand. Its sources are mainly coal and natural gas. The expectation is that all of these sectors will need more energy in coming years. In fact, total U.S. energy consumption is expected to grow by more than 18 percent by 2030.

The United States' fossil fuel addiction also weakens its national security. "America is addicted to oil, which is often imported from unstable parts of the world,"[5] former president George W. Bush stated in 2006. The United States gets much of its oil from unstable regions at high prices. This use increases U.S. military spending because the country must station troops at overseas pipelines to protect them from terrorists. Additionally, the U.S. Navy patrols sea routes, in the Persian Gulf, for example, to protect ships that deliver oil to the United States. For this

> " The world's dependence on fossil fuels is troubling to many because fossil fuels are nonrenewable resources. "

and other reasons, the U.S. government is looking for other fuel sources to lessen its dependence on oil.

Other Concerns About Fossil Fuel Dependence

In addition to being nonrenewable, there are other major issues with fossil fuels. One is cost. Fossil fuel costs, particularly oil, are unpredictable. Costs rise and fall depending on demand and reserves available. For 6 years in a row, until the summer of 2008, oil prices consistently rose. In the months following, oil prices significantly dropped. There are many factors that affect oil prices. One is OPEC. OPEC can, and has, affected the price of oil by restricting oil output. Sharp oil price swings affect businesses' and individuals' energy costs.

> "The United States is home to 5 percent of the world's population, yet consumes 26 percent of the world's energy."

Another problem with fossil fuel dependence is the major harm fossil fuel use does to the environment. Burning fossil fuels produces around 21.3 billion tons (19.3 billion metric tons) of carbon dioxide per year. Estimates indicate that natural processes can only absorb about half that amount. This leads to a net increase of 11.7 billion tons (10.65 billion metric tons) of atmospheric carbon dioxide per year. Carbon dioxide is a greenhouse gas that contributes to global warming. Scientists believe global warming causes adverse effects to ecosystems around the world.

Biofuels as an Alternative

In the United States biofuel use has significantly increased in the past 2 decades. Biofuels are now the largest domestic source of American renewable energy. Biofuels are used for car fuel, to heat buildings, and to create electricity. In 1985 the United States produced just 175 million gallons (662 million L) of ethanol. By 2007 this had increased to 6.5 billion gallons (24.6 billion L). Additionally, biodiesel consumption in the United States grew from 25 million gallons (94.6 million L) in 2004 to 450 million gallons (1.7 billion L) in 2007.

In 2007 the United States passed the Energy Independence and Security Act that requires the increasing use of biofuels. The total amount of biofuels added to gasoline must increase to 36 billion gallons (136 billion L) by 2022, from 4.7 billion gallons (17.8 billion L) in 2007.

Worldwide, biofuel use is also increasing. Along with the United States, the European Union, Japan, and China have also passed laws that mandate biofuel use. Because of these laws, the world is producing and using more biofuels. According to a United Nations report, global production of biofuels doubled from 2002 to 2007 and will likely double again by 2011.

Cars and Biofuels

Transportation is one of the main uses of biofuels. In the United States transportation accounts for about 30 percent of energy consumption. If biofuels can replace a significant amount of fossil fuels for transportation, the United States can reduce a good part of its overall fossil fuel use.

Ethanol is the most common biofuel used for vehicles in the United States. E10, a 10 percent ethanol and 90 percent gasoline blend, is sold at gas stations all over the United States. It can be used in regular vehicles. Additionally, the National Ethanol Vehicle Coalition estimates that 6 million cars in the United States are capable of running on E85. This is a combination of 85 percent ethanol and 15 percent unleaded gasoline. Because of E10 and E85 use, U.S. vehicles get about 2 percent of their fuel from ethanol.

Brazil has one of the most successful biofuel programs for vehicles. Nearly 50 percent of Brazil's car fuel comes from biofuels. In 1976 the Brazilian government made it mandatory to blend gasoline with ethanol. The mandatory blend is 25 percent ethanol and 75 percent gasoline. All cars in Brazil can be fueled with this. Additionally, the Brazilian car industry produces vehicles that can run on pure ethanol. Today more than 70 percent of the new cars sold in Brazil are flex-fuel, which means they can run on blends or on pure ethanol.

> " Along with the United States, the European Union, Japan, and China have also passed laws that mandate biofuel use. "

In Europe, the most prevalent renewable vehicle fuel is biodiesel. This is because biodiesel can be made from vegetable oils, such as rapeseed. In Europe, rapeseed is more commonly grown than sugarcane or corn, which are used to make ethanol. In the European Union, total biodiesel production in 2007 was over 6.3 million tons (5.7 million metric tons), which was an increase of 16.8 percent from 2006. Biodiesel is now available at many service stations in Europe.

Biofueled Electricity

In 2003 the East Kentucky Power Cooperative (EKPC) announced the official opening of a $4 million methane power plant in Boone County, Kentucky. Methane is a biofuel produced from waste gas from animals, landfills, and plants. A methane power plant uses methane, as opposed to coal or other fossil fuels, to produce electricity. By 2008 EKPC had opened four other plants, with a sixth planned for 2009. Together all of the plants power 8,000 Kentucky homes.

More companies have followed EKPC's lead. In 2007 the Biofuels Power Corporation began producing and selling electricity to the Electric Reliability Council of Texas power grid. The power comes from its biodiesel-powered generating plant in Oak Ridge North, Texas. The Oak Ridge North facility has a capacity of up to 5 megawatts and uses 3 diesel-powered generators. These generators run entirely on biodiesel fuel. The company opened a second biodiesel plant in 2008. Together, both plants provide approximately 9,000 homes with electricity.

> **Methane is a biofuel produced from waste gas from animals, landfills, and plants.**

Throughout the world, the biopower capacity, electricity powered from biofuels, grew at a rate of 8.3 percent between 2001 and 2007. Although this represents a significant increase of biopower capacity, the amount of the world's electricity supplied by biofuels is small. This is because of biopower limitations. Biomass power boilers are less efficient than coal-fueled plants. A lower efficiency results in higher costs for biopower companies. This deters power companies from building biopower plants instead of more lucrative coal-powered plants. However, analysts are optimistic about the future. "Most analysts believe that the economics of bioenergy will improve as larger plants are constructed with higher efficiencies," states the Northeast Sustainable Energy Association. "Increasing efficiency is the key to lowering the overall costs of bioenergy."[6]

Heating Homes with Biofuels

Biofuel heating is becoming more common in the United States. In 2008 Massachusetts governor Deval Patrick signed the state's Clean Energy Biofuels Act. This requires that a minimum percentage of biofuel as a component of home heating fuel be sold in the state. Heating fuels will require a biofuel component of 2 percent in 2010 and 5 percent by 2013. "This new law solidifies our position as a leading producer of fuel alternatives and firmly sets Massachusetts on the transitional course from fossil fuels to clean-energy products,"[7] Patrick said.

Other states are considering similar laws. However, there are factors that limit people from choosing biodiesel heating. One is price. In November 2008 a biodiesel called B100 was selling for $3.10 a gallon as opposed to $2.75 a gallon for regular heating oil. One reason for the higher cost is that pipelines cannot be used to transmit biodiesel. Instead, trucks and other vehicles transport it. Pipeline transport is cheaper. "We're working very hard at the National Biodiesel Board, with assistance from many of the national pipeline organizations, to get biodiesel approved for use in pipes," Paul Nazzaro, president of Advanced Fuel Solutions, stated. "We feel very comfortable that a 5 percent blend in the pipe is OK."[8] Before pipeline shipments can begin, it has to be determined that biodiesel blends will not contaminate other products, such as jet fuel, that are shipped through the pipeline networks.

> In 1976 the Brazilian government made it mandatory to blend gasoline with ethanol.

Biofuel Limitations

Although biofuels are a viable alternative to fossil fuels, there are many limitations. For one thing current biofuel usage cannot replace all, or even half, of fossil fuel usage. This is because of the amount of biomass required to produce needed energy. For example, even if the United States used all of its corn to make ethanol, it still would only replace 12 percent of its current gasoline use. If the United States also used all of its soybeans to make ethanol, this would only replace an additional 6 percent of the gas usage.

Another limitation of biofuel vehicles specific to the United States is availability of the fuel. As of 2008 there were 1,900 filling stations in the United States that carried E85. This is only a fraction of the country's 180,000 gas stations. As for biodiesel, as of 2008 there were only 800 biodiesel stations in the United States. Another issue with biodiesel is that its performance in cold weather is worse than regular diesel. Vehicles that use biodiesel blends may exhibit more problems, such as difficulty starting, in winter temperatures than vehicles that run on regular diesel.

> **If the United States used all of its corn to make ethanol, it still would only replace 12 percent of its current gasoline use.**

Scientists and environmentalists believe many of these limitations can be overcome. They consider biofuels to be still in the early stages of development. New developments, such as the second-generation biofuels that do not use food crops, are being made. Other advances in production and transportation of biofuels are ongoing. All together, these advances could lead to more efficient and available biofuels.

Can Biofuels Reduce Dependence on Fossil Fuels?

66 In comparison to fossil fuels such as natural gas and coal, which take millions of years to be produced, biomass is easy to grow, collect, utilize and replace quickly without depleting natural resources. 99

—U.S. Department of Energy Biomass Program, "Biomass FAQs," December 8, 2008. www1.eere.energy.gov.

The U.S. Department of Energy Biomass Program is a government program dedicated to researching and promoting biofuel use.

66 Biofuels are a greenwash scam, a feel good solution for the end of cheap oil. When one considers the industrial agricultural system that is necessary for their production, biofuels are anything but sustainable. 99

—Jim Goodman, OpEdNews, "Biofuels, the Biggest Scam Going," January 3, 2008. www.opednews.com.

Goodman is an organic dairy farmer and farm activist from Wonewoc, Wisconsin.

Bracketed quotes indicate conflicting positions.

* Editor's Note: While the definition of a primary source can be narrowly or broadly defined, for the purposes of Compact Research, a primary source consists of: 1) results of original research presented by an organization or researcher; 2) eyewitness accounts of events, personal experience, or work experience; 3) first-person editorials offering pundits' opinions; 4) government officials presenting political plans and/or policies; 5) representatives of organizations presenting testimony or policy.

66 At our rate of consumption, these fuels cannot occur fast enough to meet our current or future energy demands. 99

—Eric McLamb, Ecology Global Network, "Fossil Fuels vs. Renewable Energy Sources: Energy's Future Today," 2008. www.ecology.com.

McLamb is the founder of the Ecology Global Network, an organization dedicated to educating people about ways to protect the world's environment.

66 Our dangerous over-reliance on carbon-based fuels is at the core of all three of these challenges—the economic, environmental and national security crises. 99

—Al Gore, "Al Gore's Speech on Renewable Energy," NPR, July 17, 2008. www.npr.org.

Gore is a former U.S. vice president and environmental activist.

66 While little has been done during the current administration and previous ones, the volatility of the oil markets today has resulted in politicians finally giving more than lip service to alternative energy sources. 99

—James DiGeorgia, "Bio-Fuel Market Set to Grow by 1,000%," Alternative Energy, August 5, 2008. www.alternative-energy-news.info.

DiGeorgia is the editor and publisher of the *Gold and Energy Advisor* newsletter.

66 Absent government intervention, there would be little demand for ethanol. It has a lower energy content than gasoline, it is not significantly cheaper, and it is more difficult to transport to points of sale. **99**

—*National Review* Editors, "Hungry Like the Ethanol Wolf," *National Review Online*, April 24, 2008. http://article.nationalreview.com.

The *National Review Online* is an American magazine of conservative news and commentary.

....

66 Indeed, if biofuels are going to make a substantial dent in meeting our fuel needs, processors will need to look beyond corn. If all the corn currently grown in the U.S. were turned into ethanol, it would replace only 15 percent of our annual gasoline demand. **99**

—Julia Olmstead, "What About the Land?" *Grist*, December 5, 2006. www.grist.org.

Olmstead is a graduate student in plant breeding and sustainable agriculture at Iowa State University.

....

66 America relies on oil pipelines to meet its growing energy needs; therefore, the biodiesel industry may also need to rely on the pipelines to help secure a long-standing place in the national energy landscape. **99**

—Paul Nazzaro, "Improving Biodiesel Logistic Efficiencies: Pipe Dream Turns to the Pipeline," *Biodiesel*, May 2007.

Nazzaro is the National Biodiesel Board director of petroleum affairs.

....

Can Biofuels Reduce Dependence on Fossil Fuels?

- It takes about **26 tons** (23.5 metric tons) of ancient organic material deposited on the ocean floor to make a quarter gallon (1L) of regular gasoline.

- Petroleum, coal, and natural gas supply **40, 22, and 23 percent,** respectively, of American energy needs.

- According to the Alternative Energy Web site, biofuels are capturing about **$23 billion** of the **$1.3 trillion** the United States spends each year to power cars, trucks, airplanes, trains, and ships.

- According to a 2007 University of Minnesota study, **14.3 percent** of corn grown in the United States is converted to ethanol, replacing **1.72 percent** of gasoline usage.

- The *Washington Post* reported in 2008 that Brazil and the United States account for **70 percent** of the world's ethanol production.

- The Agricultural Resource Center reports that Brazil has **33,000 gas stations** offering pure ethanol in addition to ethanol-gasoline blends.

- In 2007 U.S. ethanol use replaced the country's need to import **228 million** barrels of oil.

- According to the European Biodiesel Board, there are approximately 120 plants in the European Union, which produce up to **6.1 million** tons (5.5 million metric tons) of biodiesel annually.

- Vehicles running on biodiesel get about **10 percent** fewer miles per gallon of fuel than regular diesel.

- According to the Energy Information Administration, approximately **8 million** of the 107 million households in the United States use oil as their main heating fuel.

Global Fuel Consumption Forecast

The world's energy demand is expected to grow in the next few decades. To meet this growth, a combination of alternative and fossil fuels will be needed. This graph predicts an increase in consumption of natural gas; biomas, geothermal, wind, and solar; and coal. It predicts a decrease in consumption of petroleum.

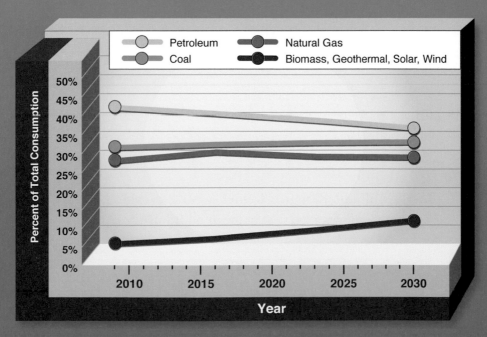

Source: Scott Tinker, Search and Discovery, "Fossil Fuels and Carbon Sequestration in a Global Energy Context. Slide 4 Global Trends," 2008. www.searchanddiscovery.net.

- Alternative energy sources, including biofuels, provide about **7 percent** of the world's energy needs, according to the Energy Information Agency.

- Biopower plants in the United States provide **1.4 percent** of the country's electric-generating capacity.

- In 2009 there were **1,590 biodiesel stations** in the United States.

Europe's Increasing Biodiesel Production

Biodiesel is increasingly being used in Europe to fuel vehicles. Germany, France, and Italy are the European Union's top diesel producers. This chart shows the increasing production of biodiesel by these countries.

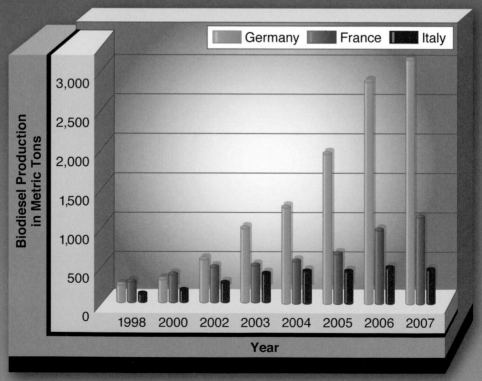

Source: European Biodiesel Board, "Statistics," 2003–2008. www.ebb-eu.org.

History of U.S. Ethanol Production

Ethanol, a biofuel typically made from corn or sugarcane, is being used around the world as an alternative fuel source. The United States is one of the world's primary ethanol producers. This graph shows the United States production of ethanol from 1980 to 2007.

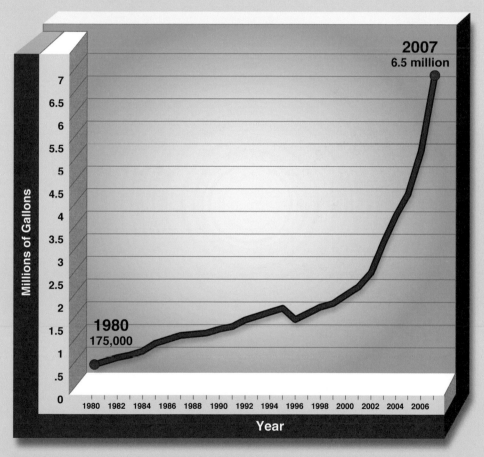

Source: Renewable Fuels Association, "Statistics," 2009. www.ethanolrfa.org.

States with E85 Stations

E85 is a mixture of 85 percent ethanol and 15 percent gasoline. As more flex-fuel cars are made in the United States there is a growing need for filling stations that carry E85. This map shows, as of 2008, which states have E85 at filling stations and approximately how many E85 stations are in these states.

States with No E85 Stations

States with 10–40 E85 Stations

States with 1–10 E85 Stations

States with more than 40 E85 Stations

Source: E85 Vehicles, "E85 Stations," 2008. http://e85vehicles.com.

How Do Biofuels Affect the Environment?

66 **Moving to biofuels will also mean cleaner air and less global warming.** 99

—The Energy Future Coalition and the United Nations Foundation, which work together to find cleaner energy options.

66 **Biofuels are a false solution to climate change and are doing much more harm than good.** 99

—Friends of the Earth UK, an environmental agency with almost 1 million supporters across five continents and more than 70 national organizations worldwide.

Much of the world is concerned about the damage fossil fuels have done to the environment. To make energy, the world burns fossil fuels. Burning fossil fuels produces carbon dioxide. The world's natural processes only absorb half of the carbon dioxide that burning fossil fuels produces. Carbon dioxide is a greenhouse gas that most scientists believe contributes to global warming.

When sunlight enters the Earth it passes through greenhouse gases in the atmosphere. These gases trap energy from the sun. Without the greenhouse effect, the Earth would not be warm enough for humans to live. However, with too many greenhouse gases the effect becomes stronger and could lead to global warming. Environmentalists and scientists warn of severe consequences from global warming, including extreme changes in temperature and weather. Some scientists believe global warming is already having an effect. "Severe droughts today affect 30 percent of the Earth's surface, compared to 10 to 15 percent 35 years ago, a change that climate scientists blame in large part on rising temperatures,"[9] writes Roger Di Silvestro, senior editor of *National Wildlife*.

These temperature and weather fluctuations can lead to damage to animals, plants, and their environments.

Environmental damage from fossil fuels is a major reason that countries are turning to alternative fuels. Research shows that alternative fuels do less damage to the environment. Of all the alternative fuels, biofuels are one of the most widely used.

Reducing Greenhouse Emissions

Both scientists and environmentalists believe that biofuels have the potential to significantly reduce the world's carbon emissions. When burned, biofuels produce carbon dioxide just like fossil fuels. However, biomass comes from plants, such as trees, sugarcane, and corn. As these plants grow, they absorb carbon dioxide from the atmosphere. This offsets the carbon dioxide emissions.

"The carbon dioxide formed during combustion is balanced by that absorbed during the annual growth of the plants used as the biomass feedstock—unlike burning fossil fuels, which releases carbon dioxide captured billions of years ago,"[10] states the U.S. Department of Energy. A National Academy of Sciences study found that using ethanol instead of fossil fuels reduces greenhouse gas emissions by 12 percent. The same study found that using biodiesel instead of fossil fuels reduces emissions by 41 percent.

> " Environmental damage from fossil fuels is a major reason that countries are turning to alternative fuels. "

However, some studies show different results. These studies have found that certain biofuels may produce more greenhouse gases than fossil fuels. A major factor is that farmers who grow biofuels often clear grasslands to grow biomass crops. A 2008 study in the journal *Science* reports that clearing grassland to grow biomass crops nearly doubles carbon dioxide emissions over 30 years. However, the same study reported that biofuels from native plants, such as switchgrass, were likely to help reduce carbon emissions. This is because grasslands were not cleared to grow these types of plants.

Do Biofuel Cars Run More Cleanly?

Many scientists have reported that biofuel vehicles run more cleanly than petroleum- or diesel-based cars. Cars that run on an 85 percent ethanol blend, E85, pollute the air less than fossil fuel vehicles. According to the Alternative Fuel Vehicle Institute, E85 reduces nitrogen and carbon monoxide emissions. These are smog-producing gases. Another benefit of E85 is that its main ingredient, ethanol, is nontoxic, water soluble, and biodegradable. This makes E85 spills significantly less environmentally harmful than gasoline or diesel.

Because of these environmental benefits, more people are buying cars that can run on E85. Since the late 1990s, Ford, GM, Chrysler, and other automakers have sold millions of flexible-fuel vehicles (FFVs) that can operate on E85. In 2007 there were 29 different E85 models for sale in the United States.

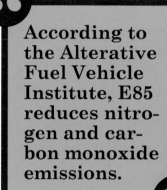

> According to the Alterative Fuel Vehicle Institute, E85 reduces nitrogen and carbon monoxide emissions.

Biodiesel also runs more cleanly than regular diesel. According to the National Biodiesel Board, biodiesel results in less carbon monoxide emissions than regular diesel. Studies at the University of Idaho also found that biodiesel spills are less toxic than regular diesel spills. The study found that biodiesel samples in water solutions were 95 percent degraded at the end of 28 days. Normal, petroleum-based diesel fuel was only about 40 percent degraded after the same 28-day period.

Biodiesel use is increasing around the world. "Because biodiesel produces fewer regulated emissions, interest in the alternative fuel is being propelled for environmental reasons,"[11] reports *NAFA Fleet Executive.* In the United States approximately 600 public, utility, and government vehicle fleets use biodiesel blends in their diesel engines.

Biofuel Production

Fossil fuels are used during the production of biofuels. Fossil fuels generate power at the plants where biomass is turned into biofuels. Fossil fuels are used to fuel the vehicles that transport biofuels. Burning these fossil fuels emits carbon dioxide. Whether or not this cancels out the carbon dioxide biomass absorbs when growing is debated.

Some scientists argue that fossil fuel use in biofuel production is small, so biofuels still absorb more carbon dioxide than they produce. The U.S. Department of Energy reports that it takes 30 to 35 percent less fossil fuel to produce a gallon of corn-based ethanol than the fossil fuel used to produce a gallon of gasoline. This means that even though some fossil fuels are burned during biofuel production, biofuels still produce less carbon dioxide than the production and use of fossil fuels.

> Recent studies show that producing biofuels such as ethanol is becoming more efficient.

Other scientific studies have different results. David Pimentel, a professor of ecology at Cornell University, and Tad Patzek, an engineering professor at the University of California at Berkeley, cowrote a 2005 report about this subject. The report stated that more fossil fuels are used to produce corn ethanol than the fuel itself actually contains. The report included the diesel fuel for the tractor that plants the corn and the energy needed at the processing plant. According to Pimentel and Patzek's calculations, it takes three times more energy to make a gallon of corn-based ethanol than a gallon of gasoline, and the gallon of ethanol contains less energy than the gallon of gasoline.

However, recent studies show that producing biofuels such as ethanol is becoming more efficient. A March 2008 report by the Argonne National Laboratory's Center for Transportation Research found that ethanol facilities in the United States used less energy and water than they did five years earlier. Additionally, they are producing more ethanol.

The Environmental Impact of Biofuel Crops

Another biofuel debate centers on whether farming practices of biofuel crops are environmentally friendly or not. Some farming practices may harm the environment. One example is the use of pesticides.

Many biofuel crops require nitrogen-based fertilizers to grow. However, bacteria in the ground consume a significant portion of the nitrogen. This is then given off into the air as nitrous oxide. Nitrous oxide has twice the greenhouse effect of carbon dioxide. This means it can offset other environmental benefits of using biofuels. "Researchers also said [ethanol] has environmental drawbacks, including 'markedly greater' releases of nitrogen, phosphorous and pesticides into waterways as runoff from corn fields,"[12] reports H. Josef Hebert of the Associated Press.

Farmers also use large amounts of water to grow biofuel crops. One study estimates that if half of the world's fossil fuel use was replaced with biofuels, the biofuel crops would need up to 2,879 extra cubic miles (12,000 cu. km) of water a year. This could create water shortages and dry up nearby lands. Drying up these lands could harm both the plants and animals within these ecosystems.

The Effect on Rain Forests

Biodiesel is made from oil that comes from plants like soybeans or palm fruit. Palm oil and soy are grown in tropical areas, which also happen to be where most of the world's rain forests grow. Many rain forests have been cleared to make room for soy and palm oil plantations. *Time* magazine reports that Brazil ranks fourth in the world in carbon emissions, and most of its emissions come from deforestation. Most of the deforestation occurs when rain forests are cleared for cattle pastures or for growing soybeans, which are used to make biodiesel.

According to environmentalists and scientists, destroying rain forests adds more greenhouse emissions to the atmosphere. A 2008 *Time* magazine article reported that deforestation, which includes both the clearing of trees and burning of the land, accounts for 20 percent of all current carbon emissions. Additionally, the destruction of rain forests kills an untold number of plants, as well as ruining habitat that animals depend on for survival. "The drive for 'green energy' in the developed world is having the perverse effect of encouraging the destruction of tropical rainforests. From the orangutan reserves of Borneo to the Brazilian Amazon, virgin forest is being razed to grow palm oil and soybeans to fuel cars and power stations in Europe and North America,"[13] writes Fred Pierce for *New Scientist.*

> " The destruction of rain forests kills an untold number of plants, as well as ruining habitat that animals depend on for survival. "

Biodiesel proponents argue that biodiesel crops are responsible for a relatively small amount of deforestation. They say that deforestation is mainly the result of illegal logging. During illegal logging, protected rain forests are cleared for their lumber. In the past decade illegal logging has increased. Between 1997 and 2005, China's forest-product imports more than tripled. According to the National Biodiesel Board, one out of every two logs China buys is illegally harvested.

Biodiesel proponents also argue that any negatives of production are outweighed by the fuel's benefits. Studies have shown that the ratio of biodiesel energy produced to the amount of fossil fuel energy used in its production is nearly four times better than that of regular diesel. Additionally, studies report that using biodiesel instead of regular diesel reduces carbon dioxide emissions by 78 percent.

Acid Rain and Air Pollution

Burning fossil fuels also releases sulfur dioxide and nitrogen oxides. When these substances are released, they rise into the atmosphere. There they mix and react with water, oxygen, and other chemicals to form pollutants that make up acid rain. Additionally, fossil fuel burning releases toxins such as carbon monoxide into the air. These create air pollution and smog.

> " Biodiesel proponents argue that any negatives of production are outweighed by the fuel's benefits. "

Acid rain is very harmful to the environment. Acid rain that soaks into the ground can dissolve nutrients that trees need to be healthy. If acid rain gets into streams and lakes, it can be deadly to aquatic wildlife. Acid rain also creates air pollution that can cause respiratory diseases in people. Using biofuels instead of fossil fuels could result in less acid rain. According to the Clean Air Organization, biodiesel emissions contain reduced levels of chemicals associated with acid rain. The overall emissions of sulfur oxides from biodiesel are 8 percent lower than from regular diesel fuel.

Air pollution is harmful to both the environment and people's health. People can develop respiratory problems from breathing polluted air.

Biofuels such as ethanol have been found to help reduce air pollutants. Some studies have found that E10 (90 percent gasoline and 10 percent ethanol) blends can reduce emissions of carbon monoxide by as much as 30 percent and pollutant particulates by 50 percent.

Is Grass the Answer?

Many environmentalists and scientists are hoping that second-generation biofuels will provide clearer environmental benefits than first-generation biofuels. Second-generation biofuels are made from nonfood crops or inedible waste products of food crops. They grow naturally, are cultivated, or come from the waste of other products.

> " Using cellulosic ethanol instead of fossil fuels reduces greenhouse gas emissions by 90 percent. "

A type of second-generation biofuel is cellulosic ethanol. It is produced from wood, grass (such as switchgrass), or the nonedible parts of food plants. According to the U.S. Department of Energy, using cellulosic ethanol instead of fossil fuels reduces greenhouse gas emissions by 90 percent. This is much higher than corn-based ethanol savings, which the Department of Energy estimates to be 10 to 20 percent. Another positive is that switchgrass yields twice as much ethanol per acre as corn. This means that less land is needed to grow switchgrass than corn. Additionally, fast-growing, high-yield switchgrass needs little fertilizer and no pesticides.

Another type of second-generation biofuel comes from the plant jatropha. Jatropha is a plant that produces seeds that contain an inedible oil. The oil is used to produce biodiesel. Forests do not need to be cleared to grow it because the plant can be grown in arid and other nonarable areas. In 2008 Air New Zealand tested a biodiesel blend made from this plant. Air New Zealand successfully tested a 400-passenger Boeing 747 jet powered partially by the biodiesel blend.

Second-generation biofuels are still several years away from commercial viability. They are not yet at the point that a significant amount of fuel can be made from them. Additionally, production is currently very costly and not efficient. However, researchers are continually working with them in hopes of creating more Earth-friendly biofuels.

Primary Source Quotes*

How Do Biofuels Affect the Environment?

66 Biomass energy uses organic matter such as wood or plants—called biomass—to create heat, generate electricity and produce fuel for cars that is dramatically cleaner than oil. 99

—Natural Resources Defense Council, "Wind, Solar, Biomass Energy Today: Biomass Energy." www.nrdc.org.

The Natural Resources Defense Council is an American action group that works to protect wildlife and the environment.

66 Realistic estimates show that making biofuels from energy crops require more fossil fuel energy than they yield, and do not substantially reduce greenhouse gas emissions when all the inputs are accounted for. Furthermore, they cause irreparable damages to the soil and the environment. 99

—Mae-Wan Ho, "Biofuels for Oil Addicts," Institute of Science in Society, February 28, 2006. www.i-sis.org.uk.

Ho is a biophysicist and a member of the Institute of Science in Society.

Bracketed quotes indicate conflicting positions.

* Editor's Note: While the definition of a primary source can be narrowly or broadly defined, for the purposes of Compact Research, a primary source consists of: 1) results of original research presented by an organization or researcher; 2) eyewitness accounts of events, personal experience, or work experience; 3) first-person editorials offering pundits' opinions; 4) government officials presenting political plans and/or policies; 5) representatives of organizations presenting testimony or policy.

66 The chief culprit in global warming is increased atmospheric carbon dioxide from industries and motor vehicles—at 372 parts per million, atmospheric carbon dioxide is now at the highest concentration in at least 420,000 years. 99

—Roger Di Silvestro, "The Proof Is in the Science," *National Wildlife*, April/May 2005. www.nwf.org.

Di Silvestro is the senior editor of *National Wildlife*.

66 Converting the grasslands of the U.S. to grow corn results in excess greenhouse gas emissions of 134 metric tons of CO_2 per hectare—a debt that would take 93 years to repay by replacing gasoline with corn-based ethanol. 99

—David Biello, "Biofuels Are Bad for Feeding People and Combating Climate Change," *Scientific American*, February 7, 2008. www.sciam.com.

Biello is the associate editor of Energy & Environment at *Scientific American*.

66 Recent research conducted at the University of Nebraska clearly shows that estimates for the energy balance of corn-based ethanol are much more favorable—in fact two to three times more favorable, than previous estimates. 99

—Cattlenetwork, "NCGA: New Research Confirms Ethanol's Growing Energy Efficiency," September 24, 2008. www.cattlenetwork.com.

Cattlenetwork provides cattle and agriculture industry news.

66 Compared to conventional diesel fuel, the use of biodiesel results in an overall reduction of smog-forming emissions from particulate matter, unburned hydrocarbons, and carbon monoxide. 99

—Energy Future Coalition, "The Benefits of Biofuels: Environment and Public Health." www.energyfuturecoalition.org.

Energy Future Coalition is an organization dedicated to promoting clean energy.

66 The real driver for clearing Brazil's precious forest is cash for wood. In the last two decades, the Amazon's contribution to Brazil's total production of tropical wood rose from 12 to 90 percent. . . . In essence, Brazil is trading its rainforest for quick cash, cattle feed, and grazing. Not for biofuels. 99

—Josh Tickell, "Where's My Orangutan? Why Biofuels Don't Kill Apes,"
Huffington Post, July 21, 2008. www.huffingtonpost.com.

Tickell is an expert in alternative fuels and consults for companies such as the National Biodiesel Board and Solar Energy International.

66 We believe that the current rush into biofuel production is misguided—it is a risky and ineffective strategy for reducing CO_2 levels and it is destroying natural habitats rich in biodiversity. 99

—Renton Righelato, "Biofuels or Forests," World Land Trust, August 16, 2007. www.worldlandtrust.org.

Righelato is chair of World Land Trust, an international conservation charity.

66 Today's biofuel industry needs to change rapidly in order to avoid worsening the climate-change problem, but doing so will put it on a path toward a sustainable and profitable future. **99**

—Alexander Farrell, "Better Biofuels Before More Biofuels," *San Francisco Chronicle*, February 13, 2008. www.sfgate.com.

Farrell is associate professor of energy and resources at the University of California at Berkeley.

Facts and Illustrations

How Do Biofuels Affect the Environment?

- According to the Natural Resources Defense Council, by 2050 biofuels could reduce greenhouse gas emissions by **1.7 billion** tons (1.5 billion metric tons) per year.

- The U.S. Department of Energy reports that corn ethanol has the potential to reduce greenhouse gas emissions by as much as **52 percent** over petroleum-based fuels.

- About **one-third** of all gasoline sold in the United States contains some ethanol.

- A 2006 National Academy of Sciences study found that ethanol yields **25 percent** more energy than the energy invested in its production, whereas biodiesel yields **93 percent** more.

- For every **107,693** square feet (10,000 sq. m) of Brazilian rain forest cleared to make way for soybeans for biodiesel, over **772 tons** (700 metric tons) of carbon dioxide is released.

- According to a 2008 Argonne National Laboratory Study, water consumption used to produce ethanol is down **26.6 percent** from 2003, and grid electricity use in ethanol production is down almost **16 percent**.

- In 2007 the biodiesel contribution to reducing greenhouse gas emissions was the equivalent of removing **700,000** passenger vehicles from America's roadways, reports the National Biodiesel Board.

Biofuels Carbon Cycle

The main environmental benefit of biofuels is that as biomass grows it absorbs carbon dioxide. Plants absorb carbon dioxide. Biofuels are made from the plants. The biofuels are distributed to fueling stations. Carbon dioxide is released into the air when they are burned. Opponents say that using biofuels causes deforestation and threatens the food supply.

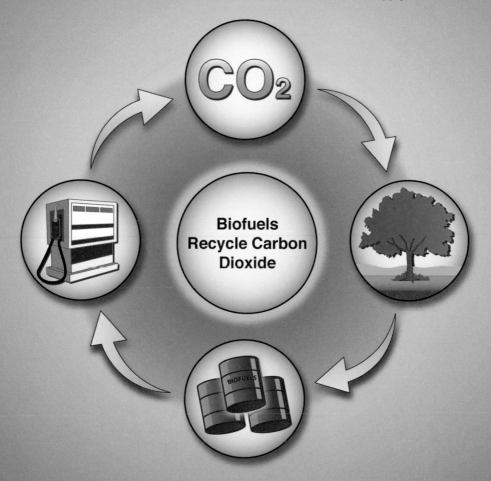

Source: United Nations Energy Futures Coalition, "The Benefits of Biofuels: Environment and Public Health," 2007. www.energyfuturecoalition.org.

- In 2008 a University of Illinois study reported that miscanthus, also known as elephant grass, has the potential to produce between **428 and 748 gallons of biofuel** per acre (4,000 and 7,000 L per ha), whereas ethanol made from wheat makes about **203 gallons** per acre (1,900 L per ha).

Biodiesel Emissions Compared with Diesel Emissions

The Department of Energy has conducted studies on biodiesel emissions. It has shown that B100 (100 percent biodiesel) emits less carbon dioxide, carcinogens, particulates, and hydrocarbons than regular diesel. The following chart shows the reduction of each when biodiesel is used instead of diesel.

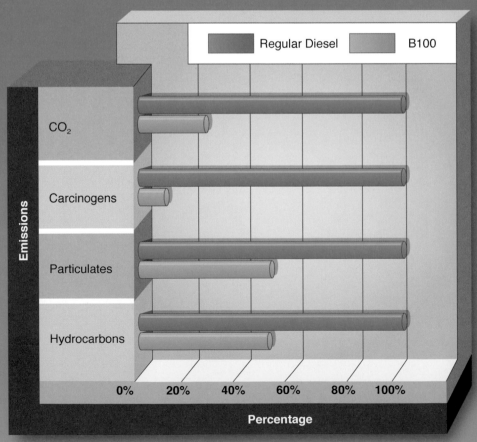

Source: Organic Fuels, "Organic Fuels: Biodiesel," 2009. www.organicfuels.com.

Pros and Cons of Biofuels

There is much debate about whether or not biofuels are really better for the environment than fossil fuels. The environmental factors depend on which biofuel is being debated. The following chart compares the environmental pros and cons of the various biofuels. It also lists whether the technology is ready for the biofuel to be used on a large scale or not.

Crop	Used to produce	Greenhouse gas emissions* Kilograms of carbon dioxide created per megajoule of energy produced	Use of resources during growing, harvesting, and refining of fuel				Pros and Cons
			Water	Fertilizer	Pesticide	Energy	
Corn	Ethanol	81–85	high	high	high	high	• Technology ready and relatively cheap • Reduces food supply
Sugar-cane	Ethanol	4–12	high	high	med	med	• Technology ready • Limited as to where will grow
Switch-grass	Ethanol	-24	med-low	low	low	low	• Won't compete with food crops • Technology not ready
Wood residue	Ethanol, biodiesel	N/A	med	low	low	low	• Uses timber waste and other debris • Technology not fully ready
Soybeans	Biodiesel	49	high	low-med	med	med-low	• Technology ready • Reduces food supply
Rapeseed, canola	Biodiesel	37	high	med	med	med-low	• Technology ready • Reduces food supply
Algae	Biodiesel	-183**	med	low	low	high	• Potential for huge production levels • Technology not ready

*Emissions produced during the growing, harvesting, refining, and burning of fuel. Gasoline is 94, diesel is 83.

**Algae has the potential for negative greenhouse emissions because of the large amounts of carbon dioxide the plants absorb while growing.

Source: *Seattle Post-Intelligencer*, "How Green Are Biofuels?" May 3, 2008. http://seattlepi.nwsource.com.

- The U.S. Department of Energy concludes that corn-based ethanol provides **26 percent** more energy than it requires for production, while cellulosic ethanol provides **80 percent** more energy.

Does Biofuel Production Threaten the World Food Supply?

66As long as [biofuels] are developed with the right criteria, and in keeping with each nation's own reality, they can be essential instruments for generating wealth and lifting nations out of food and energy insecurity.99

—Luiz Inácio Lula da Silva, president of Brazil.

66It's very hard to imagine how we can see the world growing enough crops to produce renewable energy and at the same time meet the enormous demand for food.99

—John Beddington, the United Kingdom's chief scientific adviser.

Biofuels are made from biomass. Most of today's biomass comes from food crops. The majority of these are corn, sugarcane, soybeans, and rapeseed. Grains are also used. In 2007 about 27 percent of U.S. corn was used to make ethanol. In 2006 more than 4 million tons (3.6 million metric tons) of the 47 million tons (42.6 million metric tons) of rapeseed oil produced were used in biodiesel.

The amount of food crops used to make biofuels is likely to increase. Several countries have mandated biofuel use. In the United States the 2007 Energy Independence and Security Act calls for production of 36 billion gallons (136 billion L) of biofuels by 2022. The European Union adopted the Renewable Energy Directive in December 2008. According to this directive, by 2020, 10 percent of the European Union's transportation must be powered by biofuels, electricity, and hydrogen.

To meet the mandates, a significant amount of food crops must be used to make fuel. The International Energy Agency estimates that it would take 43 percent of U.S. cropland to replace just 10 percent of American gasoline with ethanol. If half the available farmland in Germany were used to grow rapeseed, the total production would be 396 million gallons (1.5 billion L) of biodiesel. This is less than 5 percent of the total annual consumption of gasoline in Germany. People are concerned that using such large amounts of food crops to make fuel will lead to food shortages and price increases.

Food Shortages

Many people believe that the increasing use of food crops to make biofuels has resulted in people going hungry. In 2007, 8 percent of world coarse grain production and 9 percent of world vegetable oil production were used to make biofuels. At the same time there were major food shortages in countries around the world.

In 2008 food riots erupted in 18 countries, including Egypt, Haiti, and Yemen. In these countries people could not afford the price of food, including many staples such as corn, wheat, and rice. Price rises had put many foods out of reach for millions of people. The United Nations Food and Agriculture Organization warned that rising prices were triggering food crises in 36 countries. A food crisis results when a country experiences food shortages. "More than 73 million people in 78 countries that depend on food handouts from the United Nations World Food Programme (WFP) are facing reduced rations this year," reported Kate Smith and Robert Edwards of Scotland's *Sunday Herald* in 2008. "The increasing scarcity of food is the biggest crisis looming for the world."[14]

> " **People are concerned that using such large amounts of food crops to make fuel will lead to food shortages and price increases.** "

Whether or not biofuels contributed to these food shortages is a heated debate. Biofuel critics argue that any food used to make fuel is less food for people. This will only get worse, critics say, as biofuel use increases. Biofuel proponents argue that biofuels only use a small percentage of food crops. They contend that transportation costs are the main reason countries experienced food shortages. Additionally, they point out that more meat is being eaten around the world. As a result, more food crops are used to feed livestock instead of people.

Higher Food Prices

In 2008 World Bank chief Robert Zoellick announced that world food prices had risen 80 percent over the past three years. He cited this as the major reason countries experienced food crises that year. "We are seeing food on the shelves but people being unable to afford it,"[15] said Josette Sheeran of the United Nations World Food Program.

Some economists believe that food prices have risen sharply because food crops are being used to make biofuels. When fewer crops are available for human consumption, the price of food rises. From January 2005 until June 2008, corn prices almost tripled. Although wheat and rice are not used to make biofuels, their price rises are linked to biofuels. The International Food Policy Research Institute claims that the increase in corn prices led people to buy more wheat and rice instead. This demand for wheat and rice then drove up those prices. Wheat prices increased 127 percent. Rice prices rose 170 percent. According to the World Bank, biofuels were responsible for up to 75 percent of the increase.

> " In 2008 food riots erupted in 18 countries, including Egypt, Haiti, and Yemen. "

The higher prices of foods used to make biofuels also affected other foods. Corn is used to feed chickens, cows, and pigs. So higher corn prices led to higher prices for chicken, beef, pork, milk, and cheese.

The biofuels industry and the USDA argue that biofuels were not the main cause of the higher food prices. The USDA reported that biofuels only led to 3 percent of the overall food price rise. They say that the real reason for food price increases was oil. In 2008 oil prices reached new heights; the price of a gallon of gasoline rose to just over $5 in some parts of the United States. This pushed up the cost of transporting food, and increased costs such as this were then passed on to consumers.

China Restricts Biofuels

Some countries are responding to the "fuel versus food" debate by restricting new biofuel initiatives. In 2007 China banned new corn and other grain ethanol projects. It left only currently operating or under-construction projects in place.

China restricted biofuel production because its citizens' corn consumption increased. China's corn consumption rose to 165 million tons (150 million metric tons) in 2007 from 150 million tons (136 million metric tons) in 2006, and China could not meet its own corn needs. The only way to meet its food needs was to reduce the use of corn in ethanol.

> " Some economists believe that food prices have risen sharply because food crops are being used to make biofuels. "

China did not restrict the production of all biofuels. Instead, it is producing second-generation biofuels. These are biofuels made from crops that do not compete with food crops. As an example, China is researching the use of jatropha, an inedible plant, to make biofuels.

Small Farmers in Developing Countries

The biofuel industry is being touted in some circles as a means to improve incomes and food security in developing countries. Many developing countries, such as the Democratic Republic of Congo, Angola, and Kenya, have the land and climate needed to grow crops used to make biofuels. Small farmers who grow crops for biofuels, laborers who harvest them, and local people who work for biofuel companies all stand to benefit financially. This in turn would improve their food security and take care of other basic needs. "Because biofuel production is as labor intensive as agriculture, it may be a boon to rural areas with abundant labor,"[16] write Joachim von Braun and R.K. Pachauri for the International Food Policy Research Institute.

However, there are also potential problems with establishing biofuel industries in developing countries. The farms needed to grow the energy crops would require major resources. These resources include land, water, chemical fertilizers, and pesticides. Using these resources could negatively impact smaller, subsistence farmers. These farmers, often women, grow food for their families to live on. If farmers of biofuel crops use many of the local resources, such as fertilizers and pesticides, the small farmers may not be able to access these resources. As a result, their crops could fail. This would leave the farmers and their families with little food.

Sugarcane Use in Biofuel

Unlike biofuels made from other food crops such as corn and soybeans, biofuels made from sugarcane have not been touched by the food price controversy. Although Brazil is the second leading ethanol producer in the world, and it produces its ethanol from sugarcane, the price of sugarcane has remained relatively steady. And shortages of sugar have not materialized.

> Small farmers who grow crops for biofuels, laborers who harvest them, and local people who work for biofuel companies all stand to benefit financially.

This can be attributed to the small amount of sugarcane that is needed to produce a large amount of fuel. In 2006 Brazil produced 33.3 percent of the world's ethanol from its sugarcane. It used only 1 percent of the country's total farmland to grow the sugarcane needed. Sugarcane is the most efficient photosynthesizer of all plants. It can convert up to 2 percent of the solar energy it absorbs into biomass.

Despite the advantages of sugarcane ethanol, the United States does not produce much of it. This is because most of the United States does not have the climate needed to grow enough sugarcane to make a significant amount of ethanol. There is a small amount of sugarcane production in Florida, Louisiana, and, to a lesser extent, Hawaii and Texas. However, the amount they produce is less than 5 percent of Brazil's total production.

Water Use

Bioenergy crops need large amounts of water to grow. In developing countries, use of water for bioenergy crops may take water away from food crops. This could result in both food and water shortages.

India is a country with areas of water instability, and some believe that biofuels are contributing to this problem. Many Indian farmers are able to water their crops with the rain that occurs during monsoon season. However, it is difficult for farmers to plan for their crop season to exactly coincide with monsoon season. Monsoon season is not entirely predictable. As a result, farmers capture some of the rain in reservoirs and later use it to irrigate crops that grow outside of monsoon season. Already, more than 60 percent of India's cereal crops grown for food and feed production must be irrigated. The amount of crops needing irrigation is increasing as the amount of both food and biofuel crops, such as sugarcane, grows.

India is going to need more water in the coming years. By 2030 India's demand for cereal crops, grains such as oats and wheat, is also set to grow by 60 percent. Analysis shows that the amount of water needed for cereal crops will increase to 22 trillion gallons (84 trillion L). At the same time, in 2008 India enacted a new biofuels policy with a target of producing a minimum of 20 percent ethanol-blended gasoline and 20 percent biodiesel-diesel blends across the country by 2017. The biofuel crops are estimated to need as much as 5.8 trillion gallons (22 trillion L) of irrigation water. Using water for both could intensify the water scarcity that parts of the country are already experiencing. The result could be that people would not have enough water to drink or grow food crops.

Countries that grow crops for both biofuels and food are already seeing the results of increased water use for biofuels. In China, the Yellow River has lost so much water it no longer reaches the sea, and during dry months farmers in India's Punjab area must drill deeper than ever to find water. Many scientists believe biofuels are a contributing factor to these water shortages.

> " Despite the advantages of sugarcane ethanol, the United States does not produce much of it. "

Nonfood Biofuel Crops

Scientists are developing ways to produce biofuels from nonfood sources. "The only way to reap the benefits of biofuels without squeezing the food supply is to take food out of the picture," writes Joel Bourne Jr. of *National Geographic*. "Though corn kernels and cane juice are the traditional sources of ethanol, you can also make it from stalks, leaves, and even sawdust—plant by-products that are normally dumped, burned, or plowed back under."[17]

> **Scientists are developing ways to produce biofuels from nonfood sources.**

The latest biofuels can be made from nonfood parts of crops. Nonfood parts of crops include stems, leaves, and husks that are left behind once the food crops have been extracted. There are other biofuel crops that are not used for food. Examples of these include switchgrass, jatropha, and also industry waste such as wood chips and the skins and pulp from fruit pressings.

It is currently hard to extract useful biofuel from the woody or fibrous biomass of nonfood plant parts, however. These materials are mostly cellulose. Cellulose is a tough chain of sugar molecules that make up plant cell walls. Breaking up those chains and fermenting the sugars could make a lot of biofuels without competing with food crops. However, currently the process is difficult and expensive. But if researchers are able to improve this process, nonfood crop biofuels could take the food-versus-fuel debate out of the biofuel picture.

Does Biofuel Production Threaten the World Food Supply?

66 I can unequivocally state that ethanol does not take food from the mouths of starving people. Ethanol production uses field corn—most of which is fed to livestock with only a small percentage going into cereals and snacks. 99

—Toni Nuernberg, "Ethanol Promotion and Information Council Director Nuernberg: Biofuels Not at Fault in Food Crisis," Grainnet, April 23, 2008. www.grainnet.com.

Nuernberg is the executive director of the Ethanol Promotion and Information Council.

66 America's huge ethanol subsidies . . . have led to overinvestment in the businesses, which is now experiencing a sharp bust, and have helped drive up the price of food, with painful consequences for the world's poor. 99

— *Economist*, "Green, Easy and Wrong," November 6, 2008. www.economist.com.

The *Economist* is an internationally distributed magazine that contains editorials regarding political, scientific, and business news.

Bracketed quotes indicate conflicting positions.

* Editor's Note: While the definition of a primary source can be narrowly or broadly defined, for the purposes of Compact Research, a primary source consists of: 1) results of original research presented by an organization or researcher; 2) eyewitness accounts of events, personal experience, or work experience; 3) first-person editorials offering pundits' opinions; 4) government officials presenting political plans and/or policies; 5) representatives of organizations presenting testimony or policy.

66 **The impact of current biofuel policies on world crop prices, largely through increased demand for cereals and vegetable oils, is significant but should not be overestimated.** 99

—Organization for Economic Co-Operation and Development, "Biofuel Policies in OECD Countries Costly and Ineffective, Says Report," July 17, 2008. www.oecd.org.

The Organization for Economic Co-operation and Development has been one of the largest sources of comparable statistics and economic and social data for 40 years.

66 **The simple fact remains that the United States has an incredibly large amount of land, and is incredibly productive on that land. So we can afford to make both ethanol and food for ourselves, while still feeding a large portion of the world.** 99

—Brian Bals, "Food and Fuel: Rethinking the Debate over Biofuel Land Use," The Ornery American, May 29, 2008. www.ornery.org.

Bals is a research assistant in the Biomass Conversion Research Laboratory at Michigan State University.

66 **It is lack of income that fuels hunger, not the use of biofuels. Experience has proven that biofuels production generates income, increasing food consumption.** 99

—Antonio José Ferreira Simões, "Biofuels Will Help Hunger," International Herald Tribune, August 6, 2007. www.iht.com.

Simões is the director of the Department of Energy in Brazil's Ministry of Foreign Affairs.

66 [Biofuels] will also require large quantities of water—already a major constraint to agriculture in many parts of the world.99

—Charlotte de Fraiture, "Biofuel Crops Could Drain Developing World Dry," Science and Development Network, May 10, 2007. www.scidev.net.

De Fraiture is senior researcher and head of the Global Change and Environment group at the International Water Management Institute in Sri Lanka.

66 Ethanol is said to require lots of water. Actually, gasoline production uses more than 10 times as much water as does corn ethanol production.99

—Bruce Dale, "Dale Counterpoint," *Chemical and Engineering News*, December 17, 2007. http://pubs.acs.org.

Dale is a professor of chemical engineering and materials science and associate director of the Office of Biobased Technologies at Michigan State University.

66 We have concluded that there is a future for a sustainable biofuels industry but that feedstock production must avoid agricultural land that would otherwise be used for food production.99

—Ed Gallagher, *The Gallagher Review of the Indirect Effects of Biofuels*, July 2009. www.renewablefuelsagency.org.

Gallagher is chair of the United Kingdom's Renewable Fuels Agency.

Does Biofuel Production Threaten the World Food Supply?

- In 2007, according to the USDA, **229 million tons** (207.7 million metric tons) of grains were produced worldwide. Of these, almost **107 million tons** (97 million metric tons) were used to make ethanol.

- The USDA estimates indicate that **a third** of U.S. corn will be used to make ethanol by 2012.

- According to the International Institute for Applied Systems Analysis, if the biofuel industry used **716.6 million acres** (290 million ha) of available cropland worldwide, it would only meet **one-tenth** of the projected energy demands for 2030.

- In 2007 Nebraska's 16 ethanol plants consumed **a third** of the state's corn crop.

- Filling a 25-gallon (94.6L) tank with pure ethanol requires over **450 pounds (204 kg) of corn**. That much corn has enough calories to feed one person for a year, reports the Funders Network on Trade and Globalization.

- Of Brazil's **828 million acres** (355 million ha) of farmable land, sugarcane for ethanol uses **8.4 million acres** (3.4 million ha).

- According to *National Geographic*, switchgrass could produce as much **ethanol per acre as sugarcane**.

- Georgia Institute of Technology researcher Roger Webb estimates that pine groves in the southern United States could supply **4 billion gallons** (15 billion L) of ethanol a year.

From Food to Fuel

Many biofuels begin as food. This graphic shows the life cycle of biofuels.

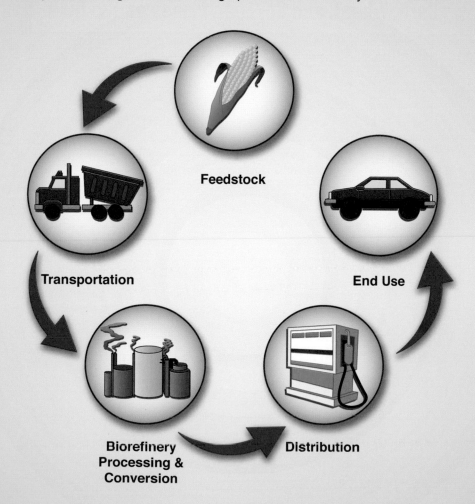

Feedstock

Transportation

End Use

Biorefinery
Processing &
Conversion

Distribution

Source: U.S. Department of Energy, "Biomass Program," April 15, 2008. www1.eere.energy.gov.

61

- Producers need **7.5 pounds** of soybeans to make one gallon of biodiesel.

- To grow enough soybeans to satisfy half the United States's diesel transportation needs, about **200 percent** of the current U.S. cropland would have to be planted in soy.

- The International Food Policy Research Institute (IFPRI) found that biofuels were responsible for **30 percent** of the rise in cereal prices from 2006 to 2007.

Corn, Wheat, and Soybean Prices on the Rise

Corn, wheat, and soybean prices have significantly increased from 1990 to 2009, and are expected to increase more. Some experts believe that the diversion of food crops to make biofuels is a major factor in the price increases.

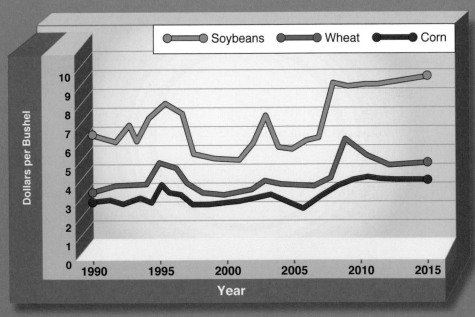

Source: USDA. "Agricultural Baseline Projections: Baseline Presentation, 2008–2017," February 2008. www.ers.usda.gov.

U.S. Crops Used for Biofuels

As biofuel production increases so does the amount of food crops diverted to biofuel use. The following graph shows the historical, current, and projected percentage of corn and soybean oil used for biofuels in the United States.

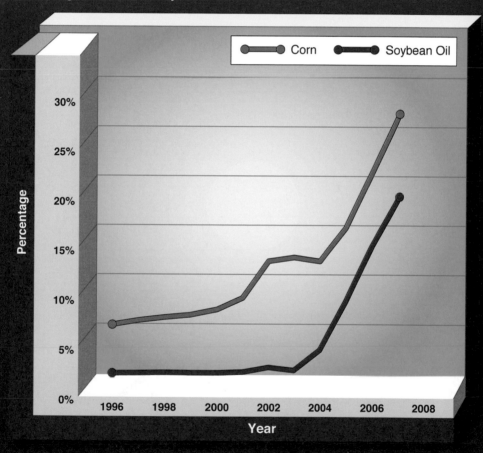

Note: 2007 levels were projected by the Food and Agricultural Policy Research Institute.

Source: Center for Agricultural and Rural Development, "Breaking the Link Between Food and Biofuels," 2008. www.card.iastate.edu.

Food Crisis Around the World

In 2008, 37 countries experienced food shortages. Some organizations, such as the World Bank, believe that biofuels contributed to these shortages because biofuels caused food prices to rise. The following world map shows which countries experienced food shortages as of April 2008.

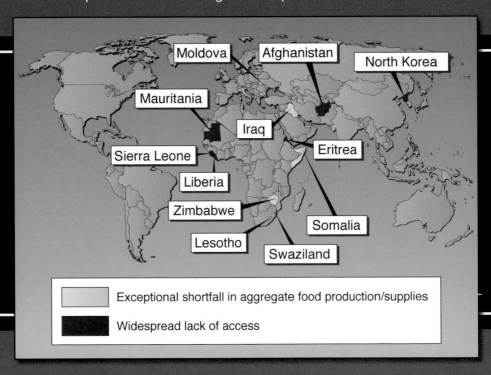

Moldova | Afghanistan | North Korea
Mauritania
Iraq
Sierra Leone | Eritrea
Liberia
Zimbabwe
Somalia
Lesotho | Swaziland

Exceptional shortfall in aggregate food production/supplies

Widespread lack of access

Sources: FAO, "Crop Prospects and Food Situation," April 2008. www.fao.org.

What Is the Future of Biofuels?

66 We need to develop and deploy the next generation of ethanol—ethanol and other products made from biomass products that are outside the food chain. In my view, this means cellulosic fuels made from agricultural waste products and crops like switchgrass, which can be grown and regenerated on less desirable lands. 99

—Samuel Boden, former secretary of the U.S. Department of Energy.

66 But let's be frank: we won't arrive at the next generation of biofuels—those that do not compete with food, threaten rainforests, or undermine communities—by just experimenting in the lab. Getting there will take big investments. 99

—Rob Routs, executive director of Shell and in charge of the company's biofuel development.

Biofuels will provide more energy to countries in the future. The United States and many other nations have adopted laws that require biofuel use. The European Union has set the goal that by 2010, 5.75 percent of its transportation fuel will come from biofuels. By 2020 this rises to 10 percent. In the United States, Congress voted to require that 7.5 billion gallons (28.4 billion L) of the nation's fuel come from ethanol or biodiesel by 2012.

Many are hoping that second-generation biofuels will meet many of these goals. This is because second-generation biofuels have several advantages over first-generation fuels. Like first-generation fuels, they are renewable, and the plants used in their production absorb carbon dioxide. Unlike first-generation fuels, however, second-generation fuels are made from nonfood crops. Second-generation biofuels can be made from crops like switchgrass and jatropha. They also are made from the discards of food crops such as rice straw from rice plants.

The difficulty with second-generation fuels is that the process to convert them into biofuels is more complex than with first-generation biofuels. Because of the production difficulties, these fuels are not cost-efficient. However, the United States and several other governments are providing funding for research to improve their production and cost.

Second-Generation Biofuel Obstacles

The major difficulty with making second-generation biofuels is getting sugars from the biomass. In second-generation biomass, it is more difficult to break down the sugars from crops than from first-generation biomass crops such as corn. To get the sugar from the second-generation biomass crops, the plants must first be treated with chemicals and enzymes. This adds time and cost to the production process.

Researchers are finding ways that could make this process easier. George Huber, an expert on biofuels at the University of Massachusetts at Amherst, and his team have developed a new way to make fuel from cellulosic biomass. It is a quicker and potentially cost-saving process.

> The United States and many other nations have adopted laws that require biofuel use.

Huber's process includes placing the solid biomass feedstocks, such as wood, in a reactor. He rapidly heats the biomass to between 752 and 1,112°F (400 and 600°C) then follows this by quick cooling. He adds a mineral, called zeolite, to the process, which helps it produce the biofuel. As a result, biofuel hydrocarbons can be directly produced from cellulose within 60 seconds. However, large-scale use of this process is not yet ready. "We've proven this method on a small scale in the lab," says Huber. "But we need to make further improvements and prove it on a large scale before it's going to be economically viable."[18]

Second-Generation Plants

Companies have started to test second-generation biofuels on a larger scale. In January 2008 KL Energy produced the first batch of ethanol from its demonstration-scale cellulosic ethanol facility. The plant is located in Upton, Wyoming. The company uses ponderosa pine waste, such as wood chips and other trimmings from trees found on the ground of the Black Hills National Forest, to make ethanol. KL Energy's cellulosic ethanol plant supplied the American Le Mans Series, a world-class sports car racing series, with cellulosic E85 racing ethanol during its 2008 season.

> "KL Energy's cellulosic ethanol plant supplied ethanol to the American Le Mans Series, a world-class sports car racing series."

More companies have also opened cellulosic ethanol plants. For example, Poet, a company that produces corn-based ethanol in plants across the United States, opened a pilot cellulosic ethanol plant in 2008. By 2009 the plant was producing ethanol at a rate of 20,000 gallons (75,708L) per year for major ethanol customers around the country. It uses discarded corncobs to make its ethanol. Poet collected cobs from 4,000 acres (1,619 ha) of farmland in 2007 and from 10,000 acres (4,047 ha) in 2008. In 2008 U.S. farmers planted 86 million acres (34.8 million ha) of corn, so there are many more corncobs out there that could be used.

Algae Biofuels

Some of the latest biofuel research involves algae. "Today, the most fervent attention in biofuel development has shifted from soil to the sea, and specifically to marine algae,"[19] reports *Science Daily*. There are several reasons that people are interested in making biofuels from algae. Algae are not used for human food, so biofuels made from algae will not affect food supplies or costs. They grow quickly and naturally in ponds; farmers can set up the ponds in ways to get the most sunlight for optimal algae growth. Algae grow fast and produce 30 times more energy per acre than land crops such as soybeans. Additionally, a relatively small amount of algae, compared with other crops, is needed to make biofuels. And, like other plants, algae absorb large amounts of carbon dioxide from the air, making them an environmentally friendly alternative to fossil fuels.

> "Tests have shown that biodiesel from algae can be a viable alternative if the production obstacles are overcome.

Biodiesel is the most common biofuel made from algae. After the algae have grown, they are harvested, and the algae oil is extracted then refined into biodiesel. The remaining material can be sold as high-protein animal feed.

There are several difficulties with producing algae-based biofuels. For example, specific strains of algae are needed to make biofuels. In open ponds wild strains of algae can develop on their own and overtake the algae strains that are being farmed. Another problem is maintaining the environmental conditions needed to grow algae. Algae do best in warm climates with lots of sunlight. This means that growing algae in open ponds limits their growth to warmer months, except in tropical areas.

Farmers can opt to grow algae in closed structures called photobioreactors. Photobioreactors enclose the algae ponds and enable the farmers to regulate the temperature and amount of light. However, the initial cost of a using a photobioreactor instead of an open pond is high because the photobioreactor must be purchased and installed. Another obstacle with producing algae is extracting its oil. An easy and cost-efficient method has not yet been developed. Currently, algae production is expensive and not yet marketable.

Tests have shown that biodiesel from algae can be a viable alternative if the production obstacles are overcome. In January 2009 Continental Airlines flew a test flight with a 50-50 blend of algae-based biofuel and standard aircraft fuel. The 90-minute flight took off from Houston and completed a circuit over the Gulf of Mexico.

Using Rice Straw as Fuel

Scientists are searching for ways to make biofuels from by-products of other industries. These by-products, such as rice straw, the stems and leaves left over after rice is harvested, are often thrown away or burned. Burning by-products like rice straw releases carbon dioxide into the atmosphere. If rice straw and other by-products could be made into biofuels, this would reduce the amount of carbon dioxide released into the air. Additionally, it would replace fossil fuels with a more environmentally friendly fuel.

Rice straw is being tested as a biofuel in China. Annually, China produces about 230 million tons (208.7 million metric tons) of rice straw left behind from its rice production. Much of the rice straw is burned, adding to China's already substantial air pollution problems.

China's initial research into rice straw resulted in the development of a straw-burning power-generation project in 2006. By the end of 2006, 34 straw-burning power plants were being built. Since then Chinese researchers have searched for other ways to use rice straw, in particular focusing on producing biomethane from rice straw. Initially, Chinese scientists had difficulty getting the rice straw to convert to biomethane in the digesters. In 2008 these scientists published a report about treating the rice straw with sodium hydroxide before using the anaerobic digester. This increased the biomethane yield by 65 percent. In 2008 three prototype facilities using this technology were built in China.

Using Landfill Gas

Much of the world's trash ends up in landfills. Part of this trash is organic waste, such as uneaten food, lawn and garden remnants, and discarded food parts such as banana and orange peels. As the organic waste decomposes in the landfill, it releases gas into the air. The landfill gas is composed of both methane and carbon dioxide, which, when released into the air, contribute to global warming. In recent years more companies have been piloting projects that capture the methane gas and use it to replace or supplement natural gas. The methane gas can be used to create electricity and to heat homes.

> " In 2008 there were approximately 435 U.S. projects that used landfill gas to produce energy for electricity and heat. "

Several companies have started to construct power plants that convert landfill gas to energy. First, landfills collect the methane gas, treat it, and then pipe the gas to the power plants. The power plants use the methane gas to generate steam and electricity.

In 2008 there were approximately 435 U.S. projects that used landfill gas to produce energy for electricity and heat. In 2009 the Virginia Beach City Council approved the permit for the construction of Virginia's first co-generation power plant fueled by methane gas. Co-generation plants produce both electricity and heat. GPC Green Energy will construct the $26 million plant at Ciba Specialty Chemicals. Skip Smith, a GPC executive, estimates the plant will reduce carbon dioxide emissions by 2,200 tons (1,996 metric tons) each year.

Currently, landfill gas is piped 3 miles (4.8km) from a nearby landfill to Ciba Specialty Chemicals. Ciba uses this to provide part of the company's power. Once the co-generation plant is constructed, Ciba will receive all available methane gas from the landfill. The co-generation plant will supply the company with virtually all of its electricity. Steam will also be produced at the plant and recycled to run systems inside of Ciba. Additionally, the plant will power 3,000 nearby homes.

More Efficient Production of Ethanol

In addition to newer biofuels, researchers are finding more efficient and environmentally friendly ways to produce first-generation biofuels. For example, Iowa State University has found a potential way to improve the process of making corn-based ethanol. Researchers have found a way to save energy and recycle more water during ethanol production.

> "Researchers are finding more efficient and environmentally friendly ways to produce first-generation biofuels.

Ethanol production begins with the dry-grind process when corn kernels are ground. Then water and enzymes are added to the kernels. The enzymes break down the starches into sugars. Next the sugars are fermented with yeasts to produce ethanol. The fuel is then used. However, there are leftovers from ethanol production. These leftovers contain solids and other organic material. Most of the solids are removed and converted into livestock feed, primarily for cattle. The remaining liquid is known as stillage. Because there are still small solids and organic material in the stillage, only about 50 percent of it can be recycled back into ethanol production. The rest evaporates.

Iowa State researchers added a fungus called *Rhizopus microsporus* to the stillage. The fungus removed about 80 percent of the organic material and all of the solids in the stillage. By doing this the remaining water and enzymes could be recycled back into ethanol production. This resulted in less waste and more ethanol produced. The researchers believe this could reduce the energy it takes to produce corn-based ethanol by one-third. Also, this process results in more water recycling. This could reduce the corn-based ethanol industry's water consumption by as much as 10 billion gallons (37.9 billion L) per year. The researchers have filed for a patent on the technology and are looking for investors to commercialize the invention.

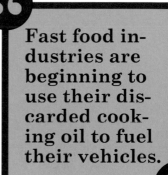

Fast food industries are beginning to use their discarded cooking oil to fuel their vehicles.

Fast Food Fuel

Fast food industries are beginning to use their discarded cooking oil to fuel their vehicles. In 2007 the McDonald's Corporation began converting its 155-truck United Kingdom fleet from diesel to B100 biodiesel. Eighty-five percent of the biodiesel comes from cooking oil collected from 1,200 McDonald's restaurants in the United Kingdom. McDonald's is also testing the use of biodiesel in the United States and Malta. Total carbon savings from the program is estimated to be the equivalent of removing 2,400 cars from the road.

Other fast food chains are following suit. Ukrops, a grocery store chain that has cafés in all of its grocery stores, recycles the soybean oil from its chicken fryers. It processes the oil into biodiesel fuel for its fleet of 15 trucks and 45 refrigerated trailers. "Ukrops expects to locally produce 50,000 to 65,000 gallons of biodiesel fuel per year,"[20] said Ukrop's director of technical services, Pat Hadden.

More companies are finding ways to turn their waste into biofuels. The advancement of second-generation fuels and more-efficient first-generation fuels will ensure that biofuel use grows in the future. Biofuel use is already becoming more common each day and is moving toward becoming an important fuel source for the world.

Primary Source Quotes*

What Is the Future of Biofuels?

66 The energy challenges our country faces are severe and have gone unaddressed for far too long. Our addiction to foreign oil doesn't just undermine our national security and wreak havoc on our environment—it cripples our economy and strains the budgets of working families all across America. 99

—The White House, "The Agenda: Energy and the Environment," January 2009. www.whitehouse.gov.

The White House Web site presents the Obama administration's positions on energy and many other issues.

66 [Second-generation biofuel] has the potential to supply a considerable proportion of low cost transport fuels if cost effective conversion processes are available. 99

—Commonwealth Scientific and Industrial Research Organization, "Second Generation Biofuels," August 5, 2008. www.csiro.au.

Commonwealth Scientific and Industrial Research Organization is Australia's national science agency.

* Editor's Note: While the definition of a primary source can be narrowly or broadly defined, for the purposes of Compact Research, a primary source consists of: 1) results of original research presented by an organization or researcher; 2) eyewitness accounts of events, personal experience, or work experience; 3) first-person editorials offering pundits' opinions; 4) government officials presenting political plans and/or policies; 5) representatives of organizations presenting testimony or policy.

> **"All biofuels are not equal. Done right, cellulosic biofuels offer a scalable and economic way to reduce petroleum use and have a meaningful impact on the environment while benefiting farmers, entrepreneurs and consumers."**

—Vinod Khosla, "All Biofuels Are Not the Same," *Washington Post*, June 16, 2008.

Khosla is the founder of Khosla Ventures, which invests in businesses, including biofuel companies.

> **"[Second-generation] biofuels are an environmentalist's dream, and could provide a very rare win-win situation for the world's energy providers. They represent a way of providing renewable energy while reducing carbon emissions, conserving biodiversity and both using and renewing otherwise degraded land."**

—Ed Yong, "How Biofuels Could Cut Carbon Emissions, Produce Energy and Restore Dead Land," Not Exactly Rocket Science, February 4, 2007. http://notexactlyrocketscience.wordpress.com.

Yong is an award-winning science writer in the United Kingdom who writes a blog that contains scientific news and opinions.

> **"Technological advances and efficiency gains—higher biomass yields per acre and more gallons of biofuel per ton of biomass—could steadily reduce the economic cost and environmental impacts of biofuel production."**

—William Coyle, "The Future of Biofuels: A Global Perspective," U.S. Department of Agriculture, November 2007. www.ers.usda.gov.

Coyle is a senior economist at the U.S. Department of Agriculture.

---

66 **The potential yields from algae dwarf those of any other biofuel crop.** 99

—Fred Krupp and Miriam Horn, *Earth: The Sequel.* New York: Norton, 2008.

Krupp and Horn are both on the staff of the Environmental Defense Fund.

66 **Unlike cellulosic ethanol, the biomass for making a lot of fuel from algae doesn't yet exist; it has to be grown from scratch. Harvesting is still expensive. Cost-effectively producing algal biofuels on a large scale may be many years away.** 99

—*Fortune*, "The Pros and Cons of Biofuels," April 24, 2008. http://money.cnn.com.

Fortune magazine provides investment information about companies and new technologies.

66 **If we dared to stand in the landfill, we would be able to identify familiar solid-waste products. . . . But what if we were able to take a really close look—down to the atomic level? We would see trillions of molecules made up of carbon, hydrogen, and oxygen, the building blocks of precious fuel to run our cars, heat our homes, and generate electricity.** 99

—Jeffrey Surma, "Finding a Sustainable Future at the Dump," *Boston Globe*, January 12, 2009. www.boston.com.

Surma is the president and CEO of InEnTec, a firm specializing in the conversion of waste into clean, renewable products.

66We must progress to the next level. That means we must accelerate the development and deployment of next generation biofuels, fuels made from cellulose, algae and from other non-food products.**99**

—Samuel Bodman, "Release of National Biofuels Action Plan," U.S. Department of Energy, October 7, 2008. www.energy.gov.

Bodman is the former U.S. secretary of energy.

Facts and Illustrations

What Is the Future of Biofuels?

- Studies conducted by the Argonne National Laboratory found that cellulosic ethanol reduces greenhouse gas emissions by **85 percent** compared to gasoline.

- In March 2007 the U.S. government awarded **$385 million** in grants to promote ethanol production from nontraditional sources like wood chips, switchgrass, and citrus peels.

- U.S. Department of Energy/Department of Agriculture reports state that there is enough biomass feedstock in the country to replace approximately **40 percent** of current U.S. gasoline consumption with cellulosic ethanol.

- The U.S. Department of Energy estimates that for algae fuel to replace all the petroleum fuel in the United States, it would require **15,000 square miles** (38,850 sq. km), which is roughly the size of Maryland.

- Soy produces some **50 gallons** (189 L) of oil per acre per year; canola, **150 gallons** (568 L); palm, **650 gallons** (2,460 L); and algae, up to **15,000 gallons** (56,781 L) per acre per year.

- Each person in the United States generates about **4.5 pounds** (2 kg) of waste per day, or almost **1 ton** (0.9 metric tons) per year, most of which is disposed in municipal solid waste landfills.

- In 2008 approximately **445 landfill gas energy projects** were in operation in the United States.

Making Second-Generation Fuels

The following diagram shows the steps of how second-generation biofuels are made. Second-generation biofuels are made from nonfood crops or inedible waste products of food crops. Land is not cleared to grow them. The process begins with plant fiber and ends up with ethanol. The process begins with the plant, such as switchgrass. Enzymes are added to the plants. The enzymes make it easier to access the plants' sugars, known as glucose. During hydrolysis, the glucose is separated from the plants. Then the glucose is fermented and distilled to make cellulosic ethanol.

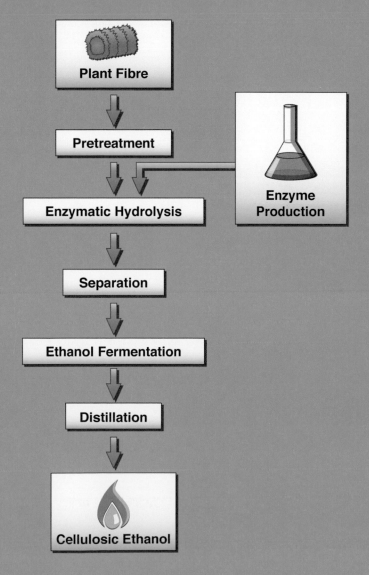

Source: Iogen Corporation, "Cellulosic Ethanol," 2005. www.iogen.ca.

- According to the U.S. Environmental Protection Agency, in 2009 there were **20 landfill gas projects** in Virginia.

- Eliminating the need to evaporate stillage would save ethanol plants up to **$800 million** a year in energy costs.

Methane Gas: From Landfills to Power Plants

Across the United States more companies are constructing power plants that are fueled by methane gas from landfills. The following drawing shows how landfill gas is captured at landfills, transferred to the plants, and converted to electricity and steam.

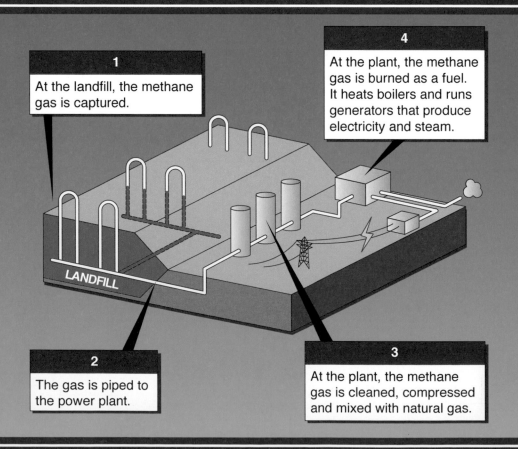

1
At the landfill, the methane gas is captured.

4
At the plant, the methane gas is burned as a fuel. It heats boilers and runs generators that produce electricity and steam.

LANDFILL

2
The gas is piped to the power plant.

3
At the plant, the methane gas is cleaned, compressed and mixed with natural gas.

Source: Scott Harper, "Permit Approved for Power Plant Using Landfill's Methane," *Virginian-Pilot*, January 22, 2009.

From Algae to Biofuels

The following diagram shows the process of converting algae to biofuels. The process begins with algae getting sunlight, CO_2, and nutrients. This algae either grows in open ponds or photobioreactors. It is then harvested and processed. The diagram shows the resulting outputs and what they create—biofuels, electricity, and other products.

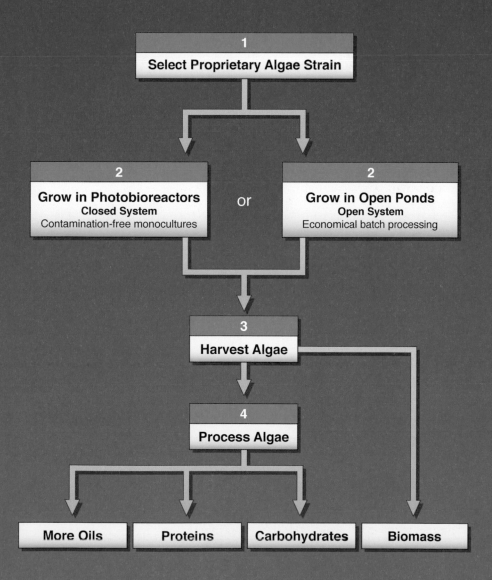

1
Select Proprietary Algae Strain

2
Grow in Photobioreactors
Closed System
Contamination-free monocultures

or

2
Grow in Open Ponds
Open System
Economical batch processing

3
Harvest Algae

4
Process Algae

| More Oils | Proteins | Carbohydrates | Biomass |

Source: HRPetroleum, "Core Technology," 2008.

Key People and Advocacy Groups

American Coalition for Ethanol: The American Coalition for Ethanol is the United States' largest association dedicated to the production and use of ethanol. It was formed in 1988 and brings together agricultural producers, farm organizations, ethanol producers, electric cooperatives, businesses, and individuals in support of ethanol. Through brochures, pamphlets, and its Web site, the organization provides information about ethanol, including its benefits, latest statistics, and current legislation. It also actively supports and promotes ethanol laws and mandates.

Samuel Bodman: Bodman was the secretary of energy from 2004 to 2009 under President George W. Bush. During his time as the Department of Energy head, Bodman promoted the use of biofuels in the United States. In 2008 the Department of Energy and the Department of Agriculture released the National Biofuels Action Plan to promote the development of a sustainable biofuels industry.

George W. Bush: Bush was the 43rd president of the United States. During his term he signed the 2007 Energy Independence and Security Act. This act mandated that the amount of biofuels added to gasoline increase to 36 billion gallons (136 billion L) by 2022 from 4.7 billion gallons (17.8 billion L) in 2007.

Steven Chu: Chu was confirmed as the secretary of energy under President Barack Obama in 2009. He won the Nobel Prize in Physics in 1997. Chu has been a vocal proponent of alternative fuels to reduce fossil fuel use. As head of the Department of Energy, Chu is responsible for maintaining the United States' energy security and upholding environmental responsibility.

Rudolph Diesel: A German inventor, Diesel invented and received a patent for the first internal combustion engine, termed the diesel engine, in 1898. A diesel engine uses compression ignition to burn the fuel, rather than ignition by a spark plug. During tests Diesel found that his engine could be run on peanut oil.

European Biomass Industry Association: The European Biomass Industry Association was established in 1996 as an international nonprofit association based in Brussels, Belgium. Its main objective is to support the European biomass industries at all levels, promote the use of biomass as an energy source, develop innovative bioenergy concepts, and foster international cooperation within the bioenergy field. It works to influence key European policies affecting the biomass industry.

Al Gore: Gore was the forty-fifth vice president of the United States. He is an environmental activist who was the presenter in *An Inconvenient Truth*, a documentary about global warming. In 2007 Gore was awarded the Nobel Peace Prize, along with the Intergovernmental Panel on Climate Change, in recognition for his efforts to educate people about and counter the effects of climate change. He has called for an end to the use of fossil fuels for American electricity production by 2018.

Lisa Jackson: Jackson became chief of the Environmental Protection Agency in January 2009. She has said her goals are to reduce greenhouse gas emissions, improve air quality, deal with the risks posed by chemicals, clean up hazardous-waste sites, and protect bodies of water from pollution. The agency assesses the positive and negative impacts of biofuels and puts forth policy based on its assessments.

National Biodiesel Board: The National Biodiesel Board is the national trade association that represents the biodiesel industry in the United States. It was founded in 1992 and promotes biodiesel research and development. It creates fact sheets, videos, magazines, and brochures about biodiesel, its production, and current statistics of use.

Barack Obama: Obama became the forty-forth president of the United States in 2009. According to his "New Energy for America" plan, he wants 10 percent of our electricity to come from renewable sources by 2012, and 25 percent by 2025. He plans to invest in alternative and renewable energy and decrease greenhouse gas emissions.

Robert Zoellick: Zoellick became the president of the World Bank in 2007. As World Bank president he works to eliminate world poverty by providing financial and technical assistance to developing countries around the world. Zoellick is critical of using food crops to make biofuels, which he believes was partly responsible for the 2008 food crises around the world.

Chronology

1796
Johann Tobias Lowitz obtains pure ethanol by filtering distilled ethanol through activated charcoal.

1908
Henry Ford produces the Model T. As a flexible-fuel vehicle, it runs on ethanol, gasoline, or a combination of the two.

1973
The Organization of Petroleum Exporting Countries stops shipping oil to the United States and other countries that supported Israel in the Yom Kippur War. This leads to high fuel prices in the United States.

1906
Under President Theodore Roosevelt, Congress passes the Free Alcohol bill, which repeals the ethanol tax. Ethanol use increases.

1945
After World War II, oil prices decrease and cause the use of ethanol to decrease significantly.

1875   1900   1925   1950   1975

1942
World War II increases the demand for ethanol, mostly for synthetic rubber and aviation fuel.

1898
Rudolph Diesel receives a patent for the first combustion engine, termed the diesel engine. During tests he discovers it can run on peanut oil.

1970
The United States passes the Clean Air Act. This allows the Environmental Protection Agency to regulate emissions standards for pollutants like sulfur dioxide, carbon monoxide, ozone, and nitrogen oxides, commonly emitted by the burning of fossil fuels.

1862
The U.S. Congress puts a $2 per gallon excise tax on ethanol to help pay for the Civil War. Ethanol use significantly decreases.

1975
Brazil forms the Pro-Álcool Program to reduce foreign oil dependence. This program uses government financing to move toward using ethanol instead of fossil fuels.

1982
The first International Conference on Plant and Vegetable Oils is held in Fargo, North Dakota. This conference deals with subjects like the effects of vegetable oil as a fuel additive.

2006
Because of Brazil's ethanol use, the country becomes energy independent. It does not have to buy petroleum from any foreign market.

2008
The European Parliament adopts the Renewable Energy Directive. It calls for a 20 percent increase in the use of renewable energy by 2020. A mandatory 10 percent goal for transportation fuels such as biofuels, electricity, and hydrogen is included in the renewable energy increase.

2005
The Energy Policy Act of 2005 contains new regulations that ensure gasoline sold in the United States contains a minimum volume of renewable fuel.

1990   1995   2000   2005   2010

2007
U.S. president George W. Bush signs the Energy Independence and Security Act. It requires the total amount of biofuels added to gasoline to increase to 36 billion gallons (136 billion L) by 2022.

2009
In Texas, Continental Airlines demonstrates the use of algae oil as an aviation fuel. In a two-hour test flight, a Boeing 737 operates with a 50 percent biofuel blend in the right-side engine.

1992
The U.S. Environmental Protection Agency passes the Energy Policy Act. This increases the amount of alternative fuel used by U.S. government transportation fleets.

2009
Verenium Corporation announces that it will construct the world's first commercial-scale cellulosic ethanol plant in Florida. It will use renewable grasses to produce 36 million gallons (136 million L) of ethanol a year.

Related Organizations

Argonne National Laboratory

Communications & Public Affairs

Argonne National Laboratory

9700 S. Cass Ave.

Argonne, IL 60439

phone (630) 252-5580

fax: (630) 252-5274

e-mail: media@anl.gov

Web site: www.anl.gov

Argonne National Laboratory is one of the U.S. Department of Energy's largest research centers. It was chartered in 1946. The laboratory has over 2,800 employees, including about 1,000 scientists and engineers. Its annual operating budget of about $530 million supports more than 200 research projects. Several of these projects focus on biofuels. The Web site provides information and papers about biofuel research and ongoing projects.

BioEnergy Science Center

Oak Ridge National Laboratory

PO Box 2008

Oak Ridge, TN 37831

phone: (865) 576-9553

e-mail: bradleymk@ornl.gov

Web site: www.bioenergycenter.org

The BioEnergy Science Center is part of the Department of Energy's Oak Ridge National Laboratory. Its mission is to revolutionize how bioenergy is processed. The center has established a team of leading experts and facilities to accomplish this. Its research is backed by more than $80 million in investments from state and private-sector sources. Its goal is to develop alternative fuel solutions that are effective and affordable options to petroleum-based fuels. Its Web site provides news, facts, and general information about biofuels and the energy they can produce.

Clean Fuels Development Coalition

4641 Montgomery Ave., Suite 350

Bethesda, MD 20814

phone: (301) 718-0077

fax: (301) 718-0606

e-mail: cfdcinc@aol.com

Web site: www.cleanfuelsdc.org

The Clean Fuels Development Coalition is a nonprofit organization that supports the increased production and use of fuels that improve air quality, reduce oil imports, and provide economic benefits to the United States. Its goal is to increase the demand for fuels like ethanol by educating and communicating with the media and supporting new legislative initiatives. Its Web site provides information about its latest initiatives, in-depth looks at biodiesel and ethanol, and publications about alternative fuels.

Environmental Protection Agency (EPA)

Ariel Rios Bldg.

1200 Pennsylvania Ave. NW

Washington, DC 20460

phone: (202) 272-0167

Web site: www.epa.gov

The EPA leads the nation in environmental science, research, and education efforts. The mission of the EPA is to protect human health and the environment. Since 1970 the EPA has been working for a cleaner, healthier environment for the American people. It studies biofuels and their effect on the environment. It recommends U.S. policy based on these results. The Web site provides detailed information about the different types of biofuels and their environmental pros and cons.

NAFA Fleet Management Association

125 Village Blvd., Suite 200

Princeton, NJ 08540

phone: (609) 720-0882

fax: (609) 452-8004

e-mail: info@nafa.org

Web site: www.nafa.org

NAFA Fleet Management Association is a not-for-profit professional society that serves the needs of members who manage fleets of automobiles, SUVs, trucks, vans, and a wide range of mobile equipment for organizations across the globe. NAFA provides its members statistical research, monthly and annual publications, regional chapter meetings, government representation, annual conferences and trade shows, educational seminars, and more. NAFA provides information about biofuels and their performance, legislation, and the latest research to its members and on its Web site.

National Ethanol Vehicle Coalition

3216 Emerald Ln., Suite C

Jefferson City, MO 65109

phone: (573) 635-8445

fax: (573) 635-5466

Web site: http://e85fuel.com

The National Ethanol Vehicle Coalition was formed in 1996. It is a nonprofit organization that is dedicated to expanding the use of E85. It also supports the increased production of flexible-fuel vehicles (FFVs) in the United States. Its Web site provides information on E85, where it is sold, who sells FFVs, and basic performance information for E85 and FFVs.

Natural Resources Defense Council (NRDC)

40 W. Twentieth St.

New York, NY 10011

phone: (212) 727-2700

fax: (212) 727-1773

Web site: www.nrdc.org

The NRDC is a nonprofit environmental action group in the United States. It combines 1.2 million members with the expert support of 350 lawyers, scientists, and other professionals. NRDC's major efforts include curbing global warming and moving America beyond oil. It supports the use of biofuels as an alternative to fossil fuels and provides advice on how this can be done. Its Web site provides information on the council's current initiatives and an annual report of their progress.

Renewable Fuels Association (RFA)

One Massachusetts Ave. NW, Suite 820

Washington, DC 20001

phone: (202) 289-3835

Web site: www.ethanolrfa.org

The RFA promotes policies, regulations, and research and development initiatives that promote increased production and use of fuel ethanol. The association is dedicated to the expansion of the U.S. fuel-ethanol industry. Since 1981 it has promoted federal, state, and local government policies, programs, and initiatives that encourage expanded ethanol use. Additionally, it is dedicated to educating the public about ethanol. The Web site provides studies about ethanol, current legislative actions about ethanol, and the industry outlook.

The White House

1600 Pennsylvania Ave. NW

Washington, DC 20500

phone: (202) 456-1111

fax: (202) 456-2461

Web site: www.whitehouse.gov

One of the U.S. president's major priorities is to implement an energy plan. President Obama has made a plan that includes investment in alternative and renewable energy, aims to end addiction to foreign oil, and addresses the global climate crisis. On the White House Web site, his energy plan, including specific goals and dates, can be accessed by the public.

World Bank

1818 H St. NW

Washington, DC 20433

phone: (202) 473-1000

fax: (202) 477-6391

Web site: www.worldbank.org

The World Bank is an international group that provides financial and technical assistance to developing countries around the world. It focuses on reducing world poverty. The World Bank has given opinions on first-generation biofuels and how they affect food shortages around the world. In 2008 the World Bank was critical of biofuels that used food crops. The Web site provides online publications about world food shortages and their potential causes.

Worldwatch Institute

1776 Massachusetts Ave. NW

Washington, DC 20036-1904

phone: (202) 452-1999

fax: (202) 296-7365

Web site: www.worldwatch.org

The Worldwatch Institute is an independent research organization with a mission to promote insights and ideas to world leaders to help them make ecologically sustainable decisions. Since 1974 it has influenced word leaders' environmental decisions. The institute's research focuses on the challenges that climate change, resource degradation, and population growth pose for meeting human needs in the twenty-first century. One of its priorities is to reduce the use of fossil fuels to lower greenhouse gas emissions. Its Web site provides information, the latest news, and opinions about biofuels and how effective they are and can be at reducing fossil fuel use and greenhouse emissions.

For Further Research

Books

David Jefferis, *Green Power.* New York: Crabtree, 2006.

David Mousedale, *Biofuels.* Boca Raton, FL: CRC, 2008.

Greg Pahl, *Biodiesel: Growing a New Energy Economy.* White River Junction, VT: Chelsea Green, 2008.

Elizabeth Raum, *Fossil Fuels and Biofuels.* Portsmouth, NH: Heinemann, 2008.

David Sandalow, *Freedom from Oil.* Columbus, OH: McGraw-Hill, 2007.

Andrew Solway, *Biofuels.* Strongsville, OH: Gareth Stevens, 2007.

Niki Walker, *Biomass: Fueling Change.* New York: Crabtree, 2007.

Periodicals

Jennifer Bogo, "The Shape of Fuels to Come," *Popular Mechanics*, September 2008.

Geoffrey Carr, "Actually There Is an Alternative," *Economist*, The World in 2009 edition.

Chhattisgarth Dhanora, "Power Plants," *Economist*, September 18, 2009.

Andrew Downie, "Brazil's Counterattack on Biofuels," *Time*, April 28, 2008.

Economist, "A Changed Climate," October 7, 2008.

———, "Sugar and Grass," December 11, 2008.

Henry Fountain, "Diesel, Made Simply from Coffee Grounds," *New York Times*, December 16, 2008.

Michael Grunwald, "The Clean Energy Scam," *Time*, April 7, 2008.

Robert Langreth, "Building Better Biofuels," *Forbes*, November 24, 2008.

Arthur Max, "Biofuel Turns to Sources That Don't Bite into Food Chain," *Virginian Pilot*, November 24, 2008.

Susan Saulny, "As Oil Prices Soar, Restaurant Grease Thefts Rise," *New York Times*, May 30, 2008.

Randolph Schmid, "Climate Has Suffered Damage That Won't Heal, Research Says," *Virginian-Pilot*, January 27, 2009.

Matthew Wald, "A Move Towards Veggie Power Aloft," *New York Times*, January 7, 2009.

Joseph Weber, "Against the Grain," *Business Week*, January 12, 2009.

Patricia Woertz, "Food for Thought," *Forbes*, November 24, 2008.

Internet Sources

Ford Motor Company, "Biodiesel." www.ford.com/innovation/environ mentally-friendly/diesel/biodiesel/bio-diesel-375p.

———, "Leading the Way with Ethanol Capable Vehicles." www.ford. com/innovation/environmentally-friendly/ethanol-e85.

Kicking Tire, "Running on Algae: To Sears Tower and Back," June 2008. http://blogs.cars.com/kickingtires/2008/06/running-on-alga.html.

Cody McCloy, "My Biofuel Road Trip: Hot as Hell, Eco-friendly," CNN, August 11, 2008. www.sidebar.cnn.com/2008/TECH/08/11/road trips.biofuel.wrapup/.

National Geographic, "Biofuels Compared," October 2007, http://ngm. nationalgeographic.com/2007/10/biofuels/biofuels-interactive.

Source Notes

Overview

1. Anduin Kirkbride McElroy, "A New Generation," *Biodiesel*, January 2008. www.biodieselmagazine.com.
2. Quoted in John Schoen, "How Long Will the World's Oil Last?" MSNBC, October 25, 2004. www.msnbc.msn.com.
3. Fred Krupp and Miriam Horn, *Earth: The Sequel*. New York: Norton, 2008, p. 72.
4. Arthur Max, "Biofuel Turns to Sources That Don't Bite Into Food Chain," *Virginian Pilot*, November 24, 2008, p. 3.

Can Biofuels Reduce Dependence on Fossil Fuels?

5. Quoted in The White House, "President Bush Delivers State of the Union Address," January 2006. www.whitehouse.gov.
6. Northeast Sustainable Energy Association, "Biopower." www.nesea.org.
7. Quoted in Massachusetts Governor, "Governor Patrick Signs Bill Promoting Advanced Biofuels," July 28, 2008. www.mass.gov.
8. Quoted in Erin Voegele, "Competition Heats Up," *Biodiesel*, January 2009. www.biodieselmagazine.com.

How Do Biofuels Affect the Environment?

9. Roger Di Silvestro, "The Proof Is in the Science," *National Wildlife*, April/May 2005. www.nwf.org.
10. U.S. Department of Energy, "ABCs of Biofuels," January 24, 2008. www1.eere.energy.gov.
11. *NAFA Fleet Executive,* "The Right Choice? Fleets Report on Biodiesel's Real-World Performance," quoted at National Biodiesel Board, September 2003, p. 1. www.biodiesel.org.
12. H. Josef Hebert, "Study: Ethanol Won't Solve Energy Problems," *USA Today*, July, 10, 2006. www.usatoday.com.
13. Fred Pierce, "Forests Paying Price for Biofuels, *New Scientist*, November 22, 2005. www.newscientist.com.

Does Biofuel Production Threaten the World Food Supply?

14. Kate Smith and Robert Edwards, "2008: The Year of the Global Food Crisis," *Laval News*, June 12, 2008. http://www.lavalnews.ca.
15. Quoted in John Vidal, "Crop Switch Worsens Global Food Prices," *Guardian*, April 5, 2008. www.guardian.co.uk.
16. Joachim von Braun and R.K. Pachauri, "The Promises and Challenges of Biofuels for the Poor in Developing Countries," International Food Policy Research Institute, November 2006. www.ifpri.org.
17. Joel Bourne Jr., "Green Dreams," *National Geographic*, October 2007. http://ngm.nationalgeographic.com.

What Is the Future of Biofuels?

18. Quoted in *Energy Daily*, "New Method Rapidly Produces Low-Cost Biofuels from Wood, Grass," April 14, 2008. www.energy-daily.com.
19. *Science Daily*, "Biofuel Development Shifting from Soil to Sea, Specifically Marine Algae," January 4, 2009. www.sciencedaily.com.
20. Quoted in *Gourmet Retailer*, "Ukrops Recycling Soy Oil into Biodiesel Fuel," June 24, 2008. www.gourmetretailer.com.

List of Illustrations

Index

acid rain, 40
Agriculture Resource Center, 30
air pollution, 40–41
algae, biofuel from
    number of acres required to replace
        U.S. petroleum fuel, 76
algae, biofuels from, 67–68
    conversion process, 79 (chart)
    potential of, 74
Alternative Fuel Vehicle Institute, 37
American Recovery and Reinvestment
    Act (2009), 6
anaerobic digesters, 10
Argonne National Laboratory's Center
    for Transportation Research, 38,
    46, 76

Bakker, Carlo, 19
Bals, Brian, 58
Beddington, John, 50
Biello, David, 43
biodiesel, 12–13, 23–24
    emissions from, vs. diesel
        emissions, 48 (chart)
    European production of, 32 (chart)
    mileage of vehicles using, 31
    reduction in emissions from use
        of, 36, 47
biofuels
    from algae, 67–68
    China's restriction on, 53
    definition of, 9
    effects on farmers in developing
        countries, 53–54
    in electricity production, 24–25
    food prices/shortages and, 18,
        51–52
    future of, 19
    global production of, 15
    growth in production of, 7
    history of, 10–11
    for home heating, 25
        number of U.S. households
            using, 31
    life cycle of, 61 (illustration)
    limitations of, 25–26
    obstacles to, 9
    pros and cons of, 49 (table)
    second-generation, 7, 72, 73
        advantages of, 65–66
        obstacles to, 66
    process of generating, 77
        (illustration)
    sources of, 41
    solid, 14
    types of, 6
        potential yield per acre, 76

See also ethanol
biomass, 6, 9–10
    available in U.S., percent of
        gasoline replaceable by, 76
    as renewable resource, 15
    See also crops, biofuel
biomethane, 9–10, 13–14
    from rice straw, 69
Boden, Samuel, 65
Bodman, Samuel, 75
Bourne, Joel, Jr., 55–56
Brazil
    ethanol production in, 12, 23, 54
    farmable land used for sugarcane
        ethanol crops, 60
    number of gas stations offering
        ethanol in, 30

carbon dioxide (CO_2), 7, 35
    annual production from fossil fuel
        burning, 22
    atmospheric levels of, 43
    biofuel recycling of, 47 (chart)
Cattlenetwork, 43
China
    restriction on biofuels in, 53
    testing of rice straw for energy
        production in, 69
Clean Air Organization, 40
coal, 20–21
Commonwealth Scientific and
    Industrial Research Organization,
    72
cooking oil, as source of biofuels, 71
corn, 60
    biofuels and price of, 52
    ethanol from, U.S. production of,
        12, 15
    percentage of U.S. crop used for
        biofuels, 30, 63 (chart)
    price of, trend in, 62 (chart)
Coyle, William, 73
crops, biofuel
    clearing of grasslands for, 36
    environmental impact of, 38–39
    major types of, 50
    nonfood, 55–56
    rain forests cleared for, 39–40
    water use and, 54–55

Dale, Bruce, 59
De Fraiture, Charlotte, 59
Department of Agriculture, U.S.
    (USDA), 52
    on global increase in food prices
        from use of biofuels, 18

on worldwide grain/ethanol
    production, 60
Department of Energy, U.S. (DOE),
    8, 36, 76
    on benefits of biomass, 27
    on cellulosic ethanol, 41, 49
    on fossil fuel use in biofuels
        production, 38
    on number of acres required to
        replace U.S. petroleum fuel
        with algae biofuel, 76
    on percent of gasoline replaceable
        by available biomass feedstock,
        76
    on potential of corn-based ethanol
        to reduce greenhouse gas
        emissions, 46
DiGeorgia, James, 28
Di Silvestro, Roger, 35, 43

East Kentucky Power Cooperative
    (EKPC), 24
Economist (magazine), 57
Edwards, Robert, 51
electricity
    biofuels in production of, 24–25
    decrease in use of, in biofuels
        production, 46
energy, forecast of global consumption,
    31 (chart)
Energy Future Coalition, 35, 44
Energy Independence and Security Act
    (2007), 22
    goals of, 50
Energy Information Agency, 31
Energy Policy Act (2005), 13
Environmental Protection Agency
    (EPA), 78
ethanol, 11–12, 30
    cellulosic, 41, 56, 74
        pilot plants for, 67
        reduction in greenhouse gases
            from, 76
    corn-based, 43
    E85 blend, states with stations
        selling, 34 (map)
    global production of, 11
    reduction in air pollution for use
        of, 41
    research on more efficient
        production of, 70–71
    U.S. production/consumption
        of, 22
    U.S. production of, 33 (chart)
    from wheat vs. elephant grass, 48
Europe
    biodiesel production in, 23–24

About the Author

Leanne Currie-McGhee is the author of several educational books. She lives in Norfolk, Virginia, with her husband, Keith, and daughter, Grace.